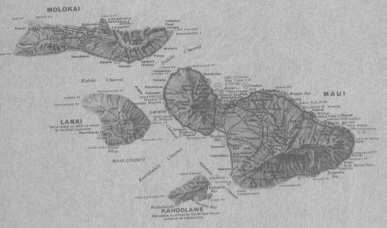

THE HAWAIIAN QUILT

楽園に咲いた布の花
ハワイアンキルト展

Curated by

Reiko Mochinaga Brandon

Honolulu Academy of Arts

Contents

目 次

ごあいさつ

　緑多い南の楽園ハワイに美しく咲いたハワイアンキルト。1800年代の初頭、ハワイをたずねたアメリカ人宣教師の妻たちによって、アメリカンパッチワークキルトの手ほどきがなされました。その後、上流社会では王族の紋章をデザイン化したフラッグキルトが生まれ、一般庶民の間ではハワイの美しい自然、特に植物をモチーフにしたアップリケキルトが多く作られました。アメリカ本土のキルトと、デザイン、技法を異にするハワイ独特のキルトは、アメリカンキルトのひとつの特異なジャンルとして、専門家をはじめ多くのキルト愛好者の間で珍重されております。

　今回はハワイを代表する4つの美術館、博物館からのアンティークキルト37点と、現在ハワイと日本のキルト界で活躍中の現代作家11人による作品15点を一堂に集めて展観する、世界初の大規模なハワイアンキルト展であります。

　本展開催にあたり、格別のご協力をくださったハワイの美術館、博物館の関係者をはじめ、現代作家の方がたに心からお礼を申しあげます。

主催者

メッセージ

　キルティングといえば、ニューイングランド地方や本土の中部、中西部の伝統あるキルトになれ親しんでいるでしょうが、実際にはキルトのフォークアートはアメリカ本土ばかりではなく、その伝統はハワイでも花を咲かせており、今日でも素晴らしい歩みを着実にみせております。

　ホノルル美術館、ビショップ博物館、ミッションハウス博物館、ドーターズオブハワイ資料館などから厳選された歴史的なキルト、並びに現代作家の作品によるこの展覧会は、ハワイアンキルトのスタイルやテクニックを余すところなく鮮明に表現しております。

　私はこの素晴らしい展覧会開催にたずさわった皆さん方に深く感謝申し上げると同時に、展示されているキルトたちこそハワイ文化の情熱そのものを誠実にお伝えしているということをつけ加えておきます。

エドワード・F・カニングハム
アメリカ大使館文化参事官

Message

　Many people are familiar with the rich American quilt traditions in New England, the South and the Midwest. In fact, the folk art of quilting has not been limited to the continental United States. The tradition has also flourished in Hawai'i, and it is most certainly alive and well today.

　This exhibition of historical and contemporary quilts from the Honolulu Academy of Arts, the Bernice Pauahi Bishop Museum, the Mission Houses Museum, and the Daughters of Hawai'i gives us a vivid selection of Hawaiian quilt styles and techniques.

　I wish to thank everyone involved in organizing this delightful exhibition. These quilts are, in their way, direct and sincere windows into the heart of Hawaiian culture.

Edward F. Conyngham

Edward F. Conyngham
Cultural Attache
Embassy of the United States of America

ごあいさつ

　過去10年ほどの間に、アメリカではキルトに対する関心が急激に高まってきました。キルトの歴史的、美術的重要性を考え、またキルトが染織美術の素晴らしい一つの分野であることを思えば、このキルトへの傾倒は当然のことと考えられます。日本では長年、染織美術が高く評価されてきましたが、その日本で近年アメリカンキルトがいくつかの展覧会を通じて紹介され、広く人びとの関心を呼ぶようになったことはさほどおどろくことではありません。しかしながら、アメリカンキルトの世界でユニークな存在であるハワイアンキルトがこれまで残念ながら展示される機会がありませんでした。

　ホノルル美術館は多年にわたり日本の関係団体と共同で数多くの日本美術の展覧会を催してまいりました。そのたびに寄せられる日本側の多大な好意に答えて、ホノルル美術館からもいくつかの美術作品が日本へ貸し出されてきました。このたび国際アートの樋口氏から日本におけるハワイアンキルト展の開催を依頼された時も、喜んでお引き受けしました。プランが進行するに従い、当美術館だけでなく、ほかの機関のキルトコレクション、および現代作品も含めるべきではないかということになり、ビショップ博物館、ミッション

ハウス博物館、ドーターズオブハワイ資料館の協力を得、このほかキルトの伝統を受けついで活躍している現代のキルターたち11人の作品も加え、総数52点、そのうち、ホノルル美術館17点、ビショップ10点、ミッションハウス6点、ドーターズオブハワイ4点、現代作品15点が出品されることになりました。これらのキルトは19世紀の後半から現代まで、その技術の高さ、そして花模様、旗、特殊なパターンなどに代表されるデザインの面白さというような点から厳選されたものです。

　この企画には、当初から多数の人びとにいろいろな形で協力していただきました。キルト選考委員会に参加をお願いした各機関の代表者、キルトの修復に協力していただいた太平洋地域コンサベーションセンターの人びと、およびホノルル美術館のボランティアの人びと、そして何人かのキルト研究者がカタログの作成にあたりました。

　最後にこの企画の担当責任者であり、ホノルル美術館染織部長ブランドン・玲子の労をねぎらうと同時に、ご協力くださったその他多くの方がたにも心からお礼を申しあげたいと思います。

ジョージ・エリス
ホノルル美術館館長

Foreword

The art of quilt making has received increasing attention in the United States over the last decade. Important for historic as well as aesthetic reasons, quilts represent one of the most exciting categories of textile arts found anywhere in the world, hence this special interest is certainly warranted.

In Japan, textile arts have been held in high esteem for hundreds of years, so it is not surprising that American quilts attracted widespread attention and praise when several exhibitions introduced them to audiences there in recent years. These presentations, however, focused on mainland quilting traditions and did not include one of quilt making's most beautiful and unique forms, the Hawaiian quilt.

The Honolulu Academy of Arts for many years has cooperated with our Japanese colleagues in the presentation of many shows in Honolulu which demonstrated the rich diversity and beauty of Japanese arts. We have benefited greatly from the generosity and enthusiastic assistance of these colleagues and have in return made modest loans from our own collections for exhibition in Japan. We were, therefore, very pleased when Mr. Toshiyuki Higuchi, Director of Kokusai Art, asked the Academy if we would plan and organize an exhibition of Hawaiian quilts for travel to various Japanese cities.

As plans progressed, it was decided that the exhibition should not be limited to works in the Academy's collection, but should include pieces from other important Hawaiian institutions as well. The cooperation and participation of the Bernice Pauahi Bishop Museum, the Mission Houses Museum, and the Daughters of Hawai'i was generously received and many fine works from their collections are included in the exhibition. In addition, it was agreed that a major component of the show should consist of quilts by contemporary Hawaiian makers, for the tradition is very much alive and current artists continue to produce works of great beauty and distinction. From these sources, a total of 52 quilts were selected: 37 historical quilts from institutions (17 from the Academy, 11 from the Bishop Museum, 5 from the Mission Houses Museum, and 4 from the Queen Emma Summer Palace) as well as 15 quilts made by contemporary artists. All of the quilts—the late 19th and early 20th century examples and the recent creations—were selected to demonstrate the superb craftsmanship of Hawaiian quilts and to show their special and diverse designs, which include royal flag patterns, varied floral patterns, and other motifs commemorating special Hawaiian events.

From the beginning of this project, many capable individuals contributed their time and expertise. Representatives of the participating institutions and invited quilt specialists served on the Quilt Selection Committee; experienced textile conservators from the Pacific Regional Conservation Center provided excellent guidance on conservation matters; each institution's textile volunteers worked many hours washing and restoring the quilts; and other dedicated individuals participated in researching and writing the catalogue. Special mention and thanks are owed to the Academy's Textile Curator, Reiko Mochinaga Brandon, whose hard work and guidance were responsible for the project's planning and implementation.

George Ellis

Director, Honolulu Academy of Arts

ほかに類をみない
ハワイアンキルトの
歴史と特徴
History and Characteristics of
Hawaiian Quilts

ホノルル美術館染織部部長
ブランドン（持永）玲子
Reiko Mochinaga Brandon
Honolulu Academy of Arts

ハワイの家の前にかざられたキルト、1900
年頃
A family's two Hawaiian quilts displayed
in front of their house, circa 1900. (Photograph courtesy of Bishop Museum)

カラカウア王の遺骸が安置されたイオラニ
宮殿、1891年
King Kalākaua lying in state, 'Iolani
Throne Room, 1891. (Photograph courtesy of Bishop Museum)

ハワイは言うまでもなく南太平洋の
真只中、緑に包まれた火山列島である。
東端の最大の島・ハワイ島から最西の
クレ島まで無人の小島を加えると、総
数132の島々が約1500マイルの海上に弧
をえがくように集列する。人が住んで
いるのは、首府ホノルルがあるオアフ
島をはじめとする8つの島々であって、
それぞれ長い移民の歴史を持ち、多種
多様の人種が共存している。政治の面
では、1898年にカメハメハ大王以来85
年継続したハワイ王国が、外部の圧力
によりやむなくその幕を閉じ、ハワイ
はアメリカ合衆国の統治領（テリトリー）として再出
発した。その後、1959年に50番目の州
としてアメリカ議会で正式に認可され
ている。

本来の慣習、伝統の面ではポリネシ
ア文化が依然として根強く残り、これ
に西欧、アジア、そのほか外来移民文
化がいり混じって、今日の特殊なハワ
イの文化背景を作り出している。

ハワイアンキルトの起源

ハワイのいわゆる「布」の歴史は19
世紀からで、ごく新しい。古くは布に
近いものとして、ワウケの樹皮をたた
いて作るカパ、パンダナスの葉を織っ
たラオハラのマットなど、自然の木の
肌を見事に利用したものが多数日常生
活に使われていた。しかし絹、木綿、
羊毛など、糸で織った布は西欧との貿
易を通して持ち込まれたものであり、
1778年、イギリスの探険家・ジェーム
ス・クックが初めてこの地に足を踏み
入れる以前、この常夏の国では全く未
知のものであった。そしてその布を糸
と針で「縫う」という技術はさらに時
を経て、1820年に訪れた宣教師一行の

妻たちによって初めて伝えられたとい
われている。その時の宣教師の1人で
あったルーシー・サーストンの残した
記録によると、1820年4月3日、ボス
トンを出港してちょうど60日目、ハワ
イ島の西を航海中であったサディウス
号の船上に、全く対象的な女性たちが
集まったという。さんさんと照る太陽
のもと、7人の宣教師の妻たちと、カ
ラクア女王を中心に4人のハワイの淑
女たちの間に鋏と糸と木綿布が置かれ、
この地始まって以来の"お裁縫"の講
習会が開かれた。この時、宣教師の妻
たちが教えた布きれを縫い合わせて作
ったパッチワークがハワイのキルトの
始まりであるといわれている。もとも
とアメリカ本土のパッチワークキルト
は、東部および中西部でその切りつめ
た生活の中で、開拓者の妻たちが古い
布の小ぎれをよせ集め、形を考え、色
を選び、丹念に縫い合わせて作ったい
わば廃物利用のベッドカバーであった。
この技術がハワイに紹介された時、余
りぎれというものがなかったハワイで
は、大きな1枚の布をわざわざ小さく
切り、またこれを縫い合わせるという
いささか本末転倒のやり方でキルトが
作られた。が、やがてそれは1枚の大
きな布を4枚または8枚に折り畳んで
切り抜き、左右対称、一連のデザイン
をのびやかにアップリケしたハワイ独
特のものへと発展していった。このア
メリカ本土のパッチワークキルトから
ハワイのアップリケキルトへの変遷が
どのような形で行われていったかは明
らかではない。先に述べたパッチワー
クのための余りぎれがハワイにはなか
ったという理由のほか、アメリカ本土

でもアップリケキルトは各地で作られたが、その数は少なく、希少価値という点からめずらしがられ、これをハワイの人たちが模倣したのではないかという説。中でもハワイのキルターたちの間に最も好まれて語りつがれているのは、木陰に干してあった白いシーツの上に、大きく影を落としてゆれ動くレフアの木の葉の模様がインスピレーションとなり、ここからハワイアンキルトが始まったという説である。いずれにせよ、ハワイのキルトのモチーフは大胆で、本土のように小さい同一のモチーフのくり返しにするデザイン構成ではない。またありとあらゆる色柄の集合体でもない。ハワイのキルトはひとつのモチーフの連続を、強い一色で、白色のうえに浮きぼりにする。シーツに使われた白い幅広の布に、ターキーレッドといわれるあざやかな赤い布を切り抜いた花模様のアップリケが、白い布一杯に広がるものが最も古い形式のキルトと言われている。これら古いキルトが圧倒的に赤を使ったという理由は、19世紀後半に移入された木綿のほとんどが赤であったからである。この後、青、緑、黄色など、ほかの原色も使われ、今日では中間色も使われるようになっているが、ほとんど原則的といっていいほど色は2色で、模様と地色の2つに限られている。柄物の布地はこれまたハワイのキルトには全く使われない。

ハワイアンキルトの特殊技法

ハワイのキルトのもうひとつの特色は、"エコー（こだま）キルティング"または"コントア（輪郭）キルティング"と呼ばれる特殊な技法である。表地と裏地の間に羊毛または木綿のわたを入れ、木綿の糸で刺し子のように一針一針縫い合わせるのがキルティングであるが、アメリカ本土のキルトはこの縫い目の線が平行斜線にせよ、または升目にせよ、原則として直線で表される。これに対してハワイのキルティングは曲線である。アップリケされた模様のまわりを、島に打ち寄せる波のようにうねうねと一定のリズムで縫い目の線がとりまく。そしてその線は水輪のように、また"こだま"のようにモチーフのまわりから、外へ外へと一定の間隔で広がりのびていく。どちらかと言えば平面的なキルトの表面にこのキルティングの曲線が複雑な立体感をもり上がらせているのである。現在のほとんどのハワイのキルトは、ハワイ語で"フムラオ"と呼ばれるこの手法で作られているが、キルトが初めて紹介された当初は、本土のキルトのように斜線、直線の縞、または升目、そのほかハワイの"カパ"のプリント模様、ラオハラマットの織り目などを模倣したキルティングが数多くみられた。亀の甲羅にヒントをえたという"クアホヌ"（亀の背）と呼ばれる独特のキルティング模様はカウアイ島で発達したといわれ、この展覧会では現代作家のジュネデイレ・クイノリスが彼女の作品"銀のつるぎ"（図版50）にその手法を使用している。キルトの縫い方も、本土のキルトは英国、ヨーロッパ手芸の影響を受け、一針一針表面から刺しては裏からまた刺すというやり方が多いが、ハワイのキルトは表面から2針か3針を続けて刺し、縫い目も多少幅広く、ゆったりしている。またハワイのキルトの場合、アップリケもキルティングも常に中心から始め、外側へと仕事を進める。本土のように、キルティングホースと呼ばれる脚つきの台を使ってキルティングをする場合もあるが、多くは全く自由に膝の上にキルトを広げ、木陰で針を進めるというハワイならではの風景の中で仕事をしている。

デザインはおもに自然がモチーフ

さて、こうして作られるハワイのキルトの最も典型的なデザインは、この地の自然、特に乱れ咲く熱帯植物の花や葉の形に基づいたものが多い。単純明快な線で表現された花模様から複雑にからみ合う花と葉のイメージまで、そのデザインの扱い方はいろいろであり、昔から親しまれている題材として、例えば"ウル"（パンの木）、"レフアの花"などがその代表的なものと言えるであろう。手の平を一杯に広げたような大きな葉と、10メートルを越える高さで知られる"ウル"は、昔からハワイの人びとの重要な食糧源として、またそのほかの生活必需品の原料としてなくてはならないものであった。こうしたことから"ウル"は"生長する"、"豊かになる"ということにつながり、今日でもキルターたちは"パンの木"の模様のキルトを作ることは自身が成長し、豊かになることだと信じているのである。またハワイ各地の山あいに咲く紅の（時には黄色の）レフアの花は古くから火の女神ペレの最も好んだ花として親しまれ、レイに作られ、また歌にもうたわれ、キルトのパターンとしてもしばしば使われてきている。こうした自然に基づいたモチーフまた

はテーマを持ったキルトにつけられた名は、大変に叙情的なものが多い。例をあげれば、この展覧会に出品されているホノルル美術館のレフアをテーマとした作品は「レフアの花にやさしく降る雨」と命名されている。そのほか「谷間のゆり」「カフルイのゆれるさざ波」「イレイレの霧」「やさしくおさえて」等々。ハワイのキルトには作家の思いをそのままに、種々さまざまな名前がつけられている。中には作者自身にしかわからないと思われる抽象的なキルト名もあるが、これは芸術一般に共通の、作品の命名は全く作家の自由ということに通ずるのではないだろうか。

ハワイ王国とフラッグキルト

こうした自然のテーマに加えて、人工的なデザインにヒントを得たものも数多くある。ハワイ王国の旗や紋章、宮殿、またその内部のシャンデリアなどの装飾品、王侯貴族の使用した冠、その他の服飾品等。中でも特筆したいのは、ハワイの旗と紋章のテーマで、これをパターンにしたキルトは "フラッグキルト" と呼ばれ、その歴史的、民族的な意味あいから、ハワイのキルトの世界では最も重要な地位を占める。ハワイ王国の旗は1816年頃、カメハメハ大王の要望によってデザインされたと伝えられるが、左上方にその当時ハワイと緊密な関係にあった英国の国旗ユニオンジャックを配し、それにハワイの8つの島を象徴する8本の白、赤、青の横縞が組み合わされている。この旗は当時初めてカメハメハ大王の宮殿の前に掲げられて以来、ハワイ王国の歴史上2度降ろされている。つまり1843

年、わずか5ヵ月ではあるがハワイが英国の統治下に入った時と、1893年、ついにハワイ王国に終止符が打たれ、クーデターに失敗したリリウオカラニ女王が退位を余儀なくされた時である。現存する大多数のフラッグキルトはこのハワイ王国との最後の決別の時に作られたもので、キルターたちが失った母国を惜しんでもはやひるがえることのない国旗と紋章をデザインにキルトを作ったといわれている。この展覧会にも多数のフラッグキルトが出品されているが、同じ旗と紋章の組み合わせでありながら、それぞれが色、デザイン、構成とも多少違い、面白いコントラストをみせている。このフラッグキルトはその性格上、神聖なものとされ、大部分は使われることなく、家宝としてそのまま大切にしまわれてきた。今日でもわずかではあるが "旗" のモチーフはキルトに生かされ、使われていて、その歴史的に特殊な意味も、ハワイ王国へのノスタルジアという形で今に続いている。

このほか歴史上の事実を記録、記念するという形で作られた特殊なキルトが少数であるが現存する。例えばカウアイ島の週刊新聞 "ガーデンアイランド" の初出版を記念したもの。同じくカウアイ島のナウィリィリ港の開港を祝うもの。ハレー彗星の出現を記録するもの等。最後にハワイのキルトデザインには人間を含む動物のモチーフはほとんどみられない。これは縁起の悪いものとして敬遠された結果であるという。

デザインの盗用と共用

ごく初期の頃にはハワイのキルトも

アメリカ本土と同じように社交の目的をかねて何人かの共同作業で作られたが、それはしだいに一貫した一人の創作へと変わっていった。特にモチーフをカットしアップリケすることはキルター一人の仕事とされる。ハワイのキルトはもともと生活の必要性から生まれたものではないだけに、装飾品、ひいては芸術品として、キルターひとりひとりの夢を実現するということが建前とされた。従って他人のキルトのデザインを盗むことはタブーであって、もしそうしたことがあるとそれとなくその事実を歌にうたってデザイン盗人を恥ずかしがらせたという話も伝わっている。しかし現実には、多くの同じデザインが、特に人気のあるパターンは何度も使われ、キルター同志の間では交換もされ、またデザイナーの許可をとってパターンを借りるというようなことも行われてきた。ただ他人のデザインを使って作られたキルトは往々にして、もとの名前でなくキルターがつけた新しい名で呼ばれることが多い。このために全く同じパターンに数種の違うタイトルがつけられている。例えば花模様と思われるパターンで「マウイの美」と命名されたモチーフは、このほか「ばらのレイ」、「ハレアカラの山頂」、「カフルイの堤防」、「エワの真珠」、「虹の端（はし）」などいろいろと呼ばれている。

作者に殉じて焼却されたキルト

ところで大部分が単独作業で作られるハワイのキルトは、一枚を仕上げるのに2000時間を要するといわれている。これはまさに愛の労作であって、多くは結婚というような儀式を経て、母か

ら子へ、祖母から孫へと贈られる。キルトを所有するということには特殊な意味があり、過去にはキルトの持ち主が亡くなるとそのキルトも焼却されて、多数の貴重なキルトが灰になった。これは故人の魂のこもったキルトをこの世に残してはその霊が安まらないという信仰からだとされている。

キルト作りの盛んなハワイ

現在のハワイでこうしたキルトの伝統を継ぐ人は一時より多くなっている。以前は一種の秘密主義から技術の"受け継ぎ"ということが途絶えがちであったが、1970年頃からキルター同志の交流、情報の交換なども盛んになり、現在はホノルルを初め、マウイ島、カウアイ島、ハワイ、モロカイ、それぞれの島でキルトの伝統はしっかりと受け継がれている。キルトワークショップもハワイ各地で開かれており、生徒の数も年々増加しているときく。中でもホノルルのカワイアハオ教会の尼僧であるメアリイ・カラマ師は、6才の頃から針を持ったというキルト作りのベテランで、アメリカの政府から伝統技術保持者としてのタイトルを贈られている。今年80才になるカラマ師の主宰する毎週木曜日、教会における無料のキルト教室には80人ほどの生徒が集まって、色とりどりのキルトを広げて楽しそうである。この展覧会では「ココナッツとパイナップル」(図版40)「謙譲の美」(図版41)の2点が出品されている。どちらも身近なハワイの自然に題材をとった。てらいのない素直な作品で、いかにも彼女の人柄そのままである。このカラマ師を筆頭に、現在活躍しているキルターたちの中から11人を選んで、彼女たちの作品15点をこの展覧会の現代作家部門で展示している。美術館所有の古いキルトから、この新しい現代への作品への移り変わりがどのようなものか、それを楽しむのもこの展覧会の企画の一つの目的なのである。会場に入ればすぐ気づかれるであろうが、古いキルトは形がややこぶりなこと、それに反して現代のものは壁面を越えるほど大きなものがたくさんある。色彩も古いものに使われた赤、青、黄など原色のみという時代からいくつかの新しい作品が示すように柔らかい中間色の導入へと、その変遷をみせている。材料の点でも昔のキルトは純木綿で素朴な味が素晴らしい。現在のものはほとんどが現代の繊維界の傾向を反映してポリエステルと木綿の混紡である。キルトを作る人たちも昔と今では大きな違いが出てきている。現代作家の名前でもわかるように、現在のハワイのキルトは人種の差を越えていろいろな人たちによって制作されている。ちなみにハワイ島のワイメアにあるキルティングクラブのメンバーは圧倒的に日系の二世、三世が多い。ハワイのキルトは旧宣教師グループとハワイの人だけのものという古くからの伝統は現在全く過去のものとなりつつあるようである。しかしながらこのクラブの一日系女性の言った言葉は今日のハワイの複雑なキルト事情の一端をよく示していて印象深い。『キルトと取りくむ時は私の一番心の安まる時。私の模様は草や花、ハワイの旗や紋章は作りたくても作りません。それはやはりハワイの人たちのもの、大切にハワイのためにしまっておきたい神聖なもの。ハワイのキルトはそういうものです』。

キルトは現在、この展覧会に出品しているホノルル美術館、ビショップ博物館、ミッションハウス博物館、クイーンエマサマーパレス（ドーターズオブハワイ）のほか、カウアイ美術館、同じくカウアイのワイオリミッションハウス、ハワイ島のライマン博物館などにも所蔵されているが、プライベートのコレクションも数多くある。

キルティングのデモンストレーションをするウルマウ村のハワイの女性
A Hawaiian woman from Ulu Mau village demonstrates quiltmaking. (Photograph courtesy of Bishop Museum)

Introduction

海辺でキルティングする女性たち
Quilting at the Hawaiian Village
(Photograph courtesy of Bishop Museum)

ハワイ新憲法発布のため宮殿を出発するリ
リウオカラニ女王、1893年
Queen Lili'uokalani leaving the legisla-
ture to proclaim Hawai'i's new constitu-
tion, Honolulu, January 1893. (Photograph courtesy of Bishop Museum)

Western influences on the culture of the Hawaiian people evolved into a distinctive type of needlework—the Hawaiian quilt. Quilt designs incorporate and reflect personal expressions of beauty, memories shared and recorded, and events commemorated and preserved. To appreciate the Hawaiian quilt, it is necessary to investigate the evolution of this unique folk art and to understand how it was influenced by Western culture.

Long before native Hawaiians had contact with Western culture they were proficient in the making of *tapa*, a bark cloth used for clothing, bedding (*kapa-moe*), and other utilitarian and ceremonial purposes. Most *tapa* was made from the inner bark of the *wauke* plant (*Broussonetia papyrifera*, or paper mulberry). *Tapa* was usually made by women who employed wooden mallets to pound the strips of bark together to form sheets of various sizes, textures, and thicknesses. *Tapa* was colored by native dyes and decorated with freehand designs applied with pronged pens.[1]

With the discovery of the Hawaiian Islands by Captain James Cook in 1778 and the subsequent arrival of explorers, merchants, whalers, and missionaries, new techniques and designs were developed and creatively adapted by native Hawaiians. Rapidly, foreign elements were integrated into the traditional culture, and Hawaiian craftsmen found that newly-introduced metal tools easily could be adapted to traditional techniques. As a result, designs and motifs soon became increasingly detailed.

Western cloth was introduced during this time as calicoes, chintzes, and Chinese silks increasingly became available through trade with the West and China. Pen-drawn or hand-printed decorations on *tapa* began to imitate the patterns of these imported fabrics. The Hawaiians also began imitating what they believed to be a superior culture by closely approximating fashionable Western clothing and accessories.

The making of patchwork quilts was introduced to Hawaiians by the wives of American missionaries. The first missionaries, who arrived aboard the brig

Thaddeus in 1820, were warmly welcomed by some of the highest chiefs of the nation. Lucy Thurston, the wife of one of these missionaries, recorded in her journal that one of the Hawaiian women had on board,

…a web of white cambric to have a dress made for herself in the fashion of those our of ladies…Monday morning, April 3rd [1820], the first sewing circle was formed that the sun ever looked down upon in his Hawaiian realm. Kalakua, queen-dowager was directress. She requested all the seven white ladies to take seats with them on mats, on the deck of the *Thaddeus*. Mrs. Holman and Mrs. Ruggles were executive officers to ply the scissors and prepare the work. …The four native women of distinction were furnished with calico patchwork to sew—a new employment to them.[2]

The missionaries' program included the teaching of sewing and other domestic arts. Sewing was initially taught on an informal basis in homes and was introduced into the school curriculum in 1830. Leftover scraps of fabrics from these endeavors were ideal for patchwork quilting, and students of both sexes were instructed in this art.

As patchwork quilting developed, Hawaiian women began to incorporate traditional and familiar *tapa* designs into their quilts. In the course of time, Western cloth, fashions, and quilts were integrated into native ways, the making of *tapa* began to decline, and by the end of the 19th century, *tapa* production waned.

It is not known exactly when the appliqued Hawaiian quilt evolved. The quilt's most striking characteristic lies in a technique which entailed cutting an overall design from a single piece of fabric which was then appliqued onto a solid-color cloth and quilted. There are different theories regarding the origin of this uniquely Hawaiian quilting method. According to a popular story, a woman set a sheet to dry on the grass. Noticing a design cast upon the sheet by the shadow of a nearby tree, she was inspired to create her quilt design.

In her study of the quilts of Polynesia, Joyce Hammond offers the following theory:

The Hawaiian applique quilt probably represents the Hawaiian modification of Western applique quilts. Such quilts did exist at the time the missionaries introduced the more practical piece-work quilt of everyday use. …There are many indications that the aura of prestige and wealth associated with the less common Western applique quilt may have influenced the Hawaiians in their selection of a quilt style to emulate. Although the methods of cutting an overall design from a single piece of fabric is unique to Polynesia, the Hawaiians may have developed their technique after seeing small Western applique designs created in a similar manner.[3]

Stella Jones, a noted pioneer in the study of Hawaiian quilts, writes:

To cut new materials into bits to be sewn together (for a patchwork quilt) seemed a futile waste of time. It was quite natural, therefore, that these women, accustomed each to her own design on her tapa beater and her own individual woodblocked patterns, should produce patterns of their own.[4]

Perhaps we shall never know exactly how or when this distinctive art form originated. Hawaiian quilts nevertheless resulted from the successful integration of styles and techniques from diverse cultures.

The techniques used in *kapa* (quilt) making followed certain progressive steps. A bright solid color was usually chosen for the appliqued design and sheeting was used for the background. In the early 1800s, Turkey red was the most common Western trade fabric available in Hawai'i and many early quilts incorporated a red-on-white color scheme. As new fabrics became available, such as chintzes, calicoes, and dotted swiss, they were incorporated into this evolving art form.

The materials were washed to ensure fastness of color. In early times, this task often was relegated to children who took the fabric to the shore and rinsed it in the ocean. If a piece of material was too small to incorporate the entire design, the piece was seamed lengthwise. The fabric was folded into eighths, and then the border and the center designs were cut. Some quilters preferred a quarter fold as opposed to the more traditional eighths; and in some cases the central design consisted of four or more separate pieces placed symmetrically around the quilt's center. Of course, the designer was not limited to such options and there were many variations of these basic guidelines.

The cut design was basted to the top sheet, starting at the center and working outward to the edges, a job often accomplished with the help of friends or relatives. As a rule, the actual applique work was done only by the owner of the quilt. The stitching used for the applique work was usually an overcast stitch. However, other types of stitching also were employed to reflect the creativity and the patience of the quilter. Batting was inserted between the top sheet and the fabric backing. Materials used for batting included soft fibers from tree fern (*pulu*), wool, cotton, and domestic animal hair.

The three layers were stitched together, again starting from the center and working outward. At times quilting was a group project; at other times quilting was done entirely by the owner. Quilting horses (large frames onto which the quilt was rolled) were set close to the ground so that the quilters could sit on mats.

The first quilting styles—parallel, circular, or diagonal lines—were those taught by the missionaries. Eventually Hawaiians incorporated stitching styles inspired by their own traditional crafts, such as the woven patterns of their mats, *tapa* designs, and motifs taken from nature, including shells, fish scales, and turtle shells. Some of these quilting styles are believed to be uniquely Hawaiian. From this point, the quilting form evolved into what is now regarded as the traditional Hawaiian technique: stitching that parallels the inner and outer edges of the appliqued design. This type of contour quilting, also known as echo quilting—called *kuiki lau* in Hawaiian—gives a three-dimensional quality to a quilt, a quality often described as resembling the waves in the ocean. Such wavelike rows of quilting (ideally measuring half an inch apart) give life to the piece and create a complementary motif.

Early applique designs tended to be fairly simple with much of the background fabric remaining visible, but before long, the designs became progressively bolder and more complex. The variety of designs was limited only by the imagination of the maker and was a matter of personal inspiration and self-expression. Early designs echoed patterns on *tapa*, but they gradually evolved in new directions, capturing the beauty of plant life and recording personal experiences, episodes of daily life, and the changing course of the Hawaiian nation. Important personal and historic incidents, symbols of the Kingdom's beloved and trusted royalty, and images evoked by dreams were memorialized.

Designs inspired by nature were probably the first and most frequently used. Quilters of each of the islands selected their own island's flowers to be incorporated into their quilts. When new plants were introduced to the Kingdom from overseas, they soon found their way into quilt designs. Also inspired by nature were designs evoking the winds and rains so vital to the islanders' livelihood. Therefore the Winds of Waimea, the Soft Rainfall of Mānoa, and the Mist of Mount Ka'ala are examples of such designs.

Historic events and personal remembrances were commemorated in the following quilts: *Manu Lawe Leka* (Carrier Pigeon) was said to record the beginning of regular mail service to the Island of Kaua'i; *Nani O Niumalu* (Niumalu Beauty) celebrated the new harbor at Nāwiliwili on Kaua'i; *Ka Hōkū Hele O Ka Pakipika* (The Traveling Star of the Pacific) recorded the appearance of Halley's Comet in 1910; *'Ehu Kai O Niakala* (Mist of Niagara Falls) memorialized a visit to those falls.[5]

Symbols of royalty signified the unquestionable trust Hawaiians placed in the guardians of their culture—their sovereigns (ali'i). Appearing in many combinations were the crowns and kāhili (royal standards), the personal adornments—fans and combs—of the queens, and the Kingdom's Coat of Arms.

A number of quilts depicted special features of the royal residences such as chandeliers found in the palace in Kona, in Queen Emma's Summer Palace in Honolulu, and hanging in the spectacular 'Iolani Palace, also in Honolulu. The 'Iolani Palace was completed in 1882 during the reign of King Kalākaua and became an inspiration for many quilters. The gaslights of the palace, the vases etched in the glass of the doors, and the torches on the grounds are depicted in quilts of that time and are still depicted in quilts today. The pavilion constructed for Kalākaua's coronation in 1883 also became a popular motif, as did Kalākaua's private residence, Haleakalā, which was built on the palace grounds.

Perhaps the most treasured of all were quilts named Ku'u Hae Aloha (My Beloved Flag), depicting the flag of the Hawaiian Kingdom. The Hawaiian Flag quilt may have appeared as early as 1843 when Lord George Paulet of the British Navy claimed possession of the Sandwich Islands (named by Captain Cook) for Great Britain. Although the British flag flew over the islands for only five months, after which sovereignty was returned, the Hawaiian people realized the tenuous status of their island nation, and it is probable that the Hawaiian Flag quilt was designed during this period.[6] There was a great resurgence in this special pattern when Queen Lili'uokalani was deposed in 1893, and when the United States annexed the islands in 1898. Although Hawaiian Flag quilts and Coat of Arms quilts appear in a variety of styles, each remains a special reminder of a Kingdom that no longer exists.

Naming a quilt was a highly personal matter. The inspiration for a particular design was not always reflected in the name given by the quilter. As they designed, many women incorporated

meanings known only to themselves, thus the name bears no relation to the subject matter depicted, and the interpretation is kept secret. Some quilts have a meaning expressed with Hawaiian subtlety, some are allegorical, and others embody a completely private meaning (kaona).

Many quilt makers guarded their designs jealously while others freely shared their patterns as a mark of friendship. A woman who shared would often do so with the understanding that every quilt made from her pattern would carry the name she had given to it.[7] Others shared their patterns with the understanding that the name of the quilt per se would be changed.[8] Today, some quilters share a design with the entreaty that the new owner change it to please herself and give it her own name.[9] Jealously guarded designs were rarely copied without permission of the owner for fear of embarrassment or shame should the "theft" be discovered.[10]

As a result of these traditions, many variations of a basic design bearing a variety of names may be found today. Over the years, the original designs, the intents of the quilters, and the original names have been lost. In such cases, a recurring theme found in the names of these quilts often gives a clue to the origin. For example, the design generically known as Ka U'i O Maui (The Beauty of Maui) has also been named Lei Roselani (Heavenly Rose Lei, the rose being the flower of the Island of Maui), Noho O Pi'ilani (Pi'ilani Ancestry, the Pi'ilani family being a royal family of Maui), Piko O Haleakalā (Summit of Haleakalā, Haleakalā being a volcano on Maui), and Kahului Breakwater (Kahului is located on the Island of Maui). From these examples it is inferred that the design originated on the Island of Maui. However, a few quilt makers had no reason to refer to Maui when naming their quilts of this design. As a result, the design also has been called Helene's Lei, The Pearl of 'Ewa (on O'ahu), and The Edge of the Rainbow. Another design with a variety of names is that of the quilt on page 123, Ka Pika Wai O Kalau Paka (The Vase of

Tobacco Leaves and Flowers). Other quilts of this design, or variations of it, are translated as Chandeliers, Light of Kahului, The Lush Growth of Mount Ka'ala (on the Island of O'ahu), and Carnations.

In most cases, the more variation on a basic design and the greater variety of names given to that particular design, the older the design is believed to be. This makes students of Hawaiian quilts curious about the origin of the design and the intent of its maker.

Today, Hawaiian quilt making is practiced with creativity and enthusiasm. New designs are created to memorialize current events, record newly introduced plants, and preserve special memories. Old designs are still used, incorporating subtle alterations that enhance the beauty of each piece, and patterns are shared with warmth and friendship. There are many quilting classes and clubs, there is a thriving commercial pattern industry, and Hawaiian quilts are prominently displayed in museums throughout the state.

Lee S. Wild

Mission Houses Museum

Notes

1. Adrienne L. Kaeppler, The Fabrics of Hawaii (Bark Cloth) (London: F. Lewis Publishers, 1975), 8.

2. Lucy G. Thurston, Life and Times of Mrs. Lucy G. Thurston (Honolulu: The Friend, 1934), 32.

3. Joyce D. Hammond, Tifaifai and Quilts of Polynesia (Honolulu: University of Hawaii Press, 1986), 14.

4. Stella M. Jones, Hawaiian Quilts (Honolulu: Honolulu Academy of Arts, 1973), 10.

5. Edith R. Plews, Hawaiian Quilting on Kauai (An Address Given to the Mokihana Club at Lihue, Kauai, March 1933), (Kauai: Kauai Museum Publications, 1976), 6, 16, 22.

6. Elizabeth Akana, "Ku'u Hae Aloha," The Quilt Digest, II (San Francisco: Kiracof and Kile, 1984), 73.

7. Dorothy B. Barrere, "Hawaiian Quilting: A Way of Life," The Conch Shell (Honolulu: Bishop Museum Association, 3, No. 2, 1965), 17.

8. Elizabeth A. Akana, Hawaiian Quilting: A Fine Art (Honolulu: Hawaiian Mission Children's Society, 1981), 43.

9. Mealii Kalama quoted in Richard J. (Tibbetts) Jr. and Elaine Zinn, The Hawaiian Quilt—A Cherished Tradition, a 16 mm film (Produced by Hawaii Craftsmen, Honolulu: 1986).

10. Roger G. Rose, Hawaii: The Royal Isles (Honolulu: Bishop Museum Press, 1980), 176.

ホノルル美術館

　ホノルル美術館はハワイの最大かつ最も古い美術館である。1927年、広い見識で知られたチャールズ・クック夫人の美術に対する情熱と、またそれをハワイの人びととわかちたいという切望から創設された。それ以来美術館は年ごとに成長し、現在ではハワイの最もダイナミックな文化と美術のセンターとなっている。

　美術館のハワイアンキルトコレクションはアメリカでは最高の一つとされ、数は26点と少ないが、作品ひとつひとつは19世紀から20世紀にかけて現地ハワイのキルターたちによって作られた逸品ばかりであり、その種類も旗のキルト、花模様のキルト、そのほか歴史上の事実を記念する特殊なキルトなど、いろいろである。こうしたキルトはハワイおよびアメリカ本土各地で展示され、数多くの出版物を通じて紹介されている。

　このほか収蔵品は、東洋、西欧、太平洋地域、アメリカ、アフリカと多岐にわたり、コレクションは世界的評価を受けている。中でもジエームス・ミッチナーの浮世絵コレクションとイタリアルネッサンスの絵画を集めたクレスコレクションは特に有名である。常設展のほか、美術館では年に約40にのぼる展覧会を開き、アカデミー劇場では400近くの映画、コンサート、講演会などが開催されている。

　美術館の建物は1925年にバートラム・グードヒュー、およびハーデイ・フィリップの両建築家によってデザインされ、アメリカ建築家協会から"ハワイで最も美しい建築物"として選ばれ、国および州指定の歴史的建物となっている。美術館は30のギャラリーが6つの庭園にかこまれ、庭に面したコーヒーショップ、劇場を持ち、はす向かいのリネコアスクールは美術館のアートセンターとしていろいろなアートクラスが開かれている。ホノルル美術館は入場無料で月曜日が休館である。

キャロル・キューホック
ホノルル美術館広報部長

Honolulu Academy of Arts

　The Honolulu Academy of Arts is Hawai'i's oldest and largest art museum. Founded in 1927 by Mrs. Charles M. Cooke, a woman of remarkable vision who desired to share her love of art with the people of Hawai'i, the Academy has grown, since its inception, to become one of Honolulu's most dynamic centers for culture and the arts.

　The Hawaiian quilt collection at the Academy is known as one of the best in the country. Although the collection is small, containing a total of 26 quilts, the pieces are well selected. Each example is a gem of the 19th or 20th century made by a local quilter from the Islands. The collection includes precious royal flag quilts, various delightful Hawaiian floral quilts, as well as unique, one-of-a-kind examples with designs commemorating special events in Hawai'i. Many quilts from the collection have been shown in important quilt exhibitions on the mainland and in Hawai'i and have been included in numerous publications.

　The Honolulu Academy of Arts' collections of Asian, European, Pacific, American, and African art have received international recognition for their excellence. Particularly noteworthy collections on view at the Academy include the James A. Michener Collection of Ukiyo-e and the Kress Collection of Italian Renaissance Paintings. In addition to its permanent collections, the Academy maintains an active and varied annual schedule featuring over forty temporary exhibitions and approximately 400 theatre events including concerts, lectures, and film and video presentations.

　The Honolulu Academy of Arts' building was designed in 1925 by architects Bertram Goodhue and Hardie Phillip. Voted by the Hawaii Chapter of the American Institute of Architects as Hawai'i's most beautiful building, the Academy is registered as both a National and State Historic Place. The museum's collections are housed in thirty galleries surrounding six garden courts, the Academy Theatre, the open-air Garden Cafe, and the Academy Shop. Located across from the Academy at Beretania and Victoria Streets is the Academy Art Center at Linekona, where a variety of studio art classes are offered to children and adults.

　The Honolulu Academy of Arts is a nonprofit institution open to the public free of charge Tuesday through Sunday, throughout the year.

Carol Khewhok
Honolulu Academy of Arts

ビショップ博物館

ビショップ博物館はカメハメハ王朝最後の王族で、銀行家のチャールス・リード・ビショップ夫人となったバーニス・パウアヒ・ビショップの死後、その残された彼女の土地と、民族学的収集品の数かずを基にして設立されたものである。1888年に着工、1891年6月22日に博物館として一般公開された。それ以来ビショップ博物館は国際的な科学、研究、教育の場として知られ、ハワイの過去と未来をつなぎ、また太平洋地域と世界を結ぶ役割を果してきた。

博物館の入場者は、20万の学童を含めて年間30万人を越え、特別な催しものや展覧会がよく知られている。収蔵品もポリネシア関係、民族資料、植物、昆虫、魚類、そのほか動物学上の資料も多々ある。

マーガリート・アシュフォード
ビショップ博物館　図書館員

Bernice Pauahi Bishop Museum

The founding date of the Bernice Pauahi Bishop Museum is officially designated as December 19, 1889, a date chosen by the Museum's trustees to coincide with the 58th anniversary of the birth of Bernice Pauahi Bishop, one of the last high ranking *ali'i* (chiefess) of the Kamehameha dynasty. Mrs. Bishop died in 1884 leaving her lands to become the basis of the Bernice Pauahi Bishop Estate. Her husband, Charles Reed Bishop—a successful and well-traveled banker—decided to create a museum for her ethnographic collection.

In 1888, ground was broken for the Bernice Pauahi Bishop Museum. The original building, constructed of locally quarried lava, is presently the site of the Museum's Kāhili Room, Hawaiian Vestibule, and the Hall of Hawaiian Natural History. Following the building's completion, the Bernice Pauahi Bishop Museum officially opened to the public on June 22, 1891.

Since that time, the Bernice Pauahi Bishop Museum has grown into an institution of international status with comprehensive scientific, research, and educational capabilities and has become a major link between the past and the future of Hawai'i, the Pacific, and the world. Grounds include the Planetarium and the Atherton Hālau where traditional Hawaiian folk crafts are demonstrated. Collections have grown to include Polynesian ethnographic, plant, insect, fish, and extensive zoological material. The Museum accomodates over 100,000 visitors annually and offers a rich variety of special events and exhibitions.

Marguerite Ashford

Bernice Pauahi Bishop Museum

ミッションハウス博物館

　ミッションハウス博物館の現在の建物は、本来キリスト教伝道のため、初めてハワイを訪れた宣教師たちの当時の教会本部と住宅を一ヵ所に集めたものである。このような教会住宅の中で、宣教師の妻たちがハワイの女性たちに、初めて洋服を作り、キルトを作ることを教えたのである。新しい、そして美しいハワイのクラフトアート作りがこうして始まり、またここから全く異なった文化と価値観を持つ女性たちの間に、新しい交流と相互理解が生まれていった。現在ミッションハウス博物館は19世紀、ホノルルで活躍した宣教師たちの生活とその仕事ぶりを示す、いろいろなプログラムを組み、一般に公開している。中でも毎年行われるハワイアンキルトの展覧会は非常に好評である。今回の意義あるハワイアンキルト日本展でミッションハウスのキルトコレクションを日本の愛好者に紹介できるのは大変喜ばしい。この機会にキルトの素晴らしさだけでなく、キルトが伝えるその当時の女性たちの生活、ひいてはその背後の文化の理解へとつながれば幸いである。

デボラ・ポープ
ミッションハウス博物館館長

Mission Houses Museum

The three historic houses which make up the Mission Houses Museum originally served as the family homes and headquarters for the first Christian mission to Hawai'i. It was in these homes, and other mission homes like them, that native Hawaiian women and missionary women first sat down to share the work of fashioning and making quilts. From these meetings grew not only a new and beautiful folk art but a new means of exchange and understanding between women of radically different cultures and values.

Today, the Mission Houses Museum offers a wide variety of programs which interpret the lives and work of missionaries and Hawaiians in early 19th century Honolulu, including guided tours, living history programs, craft and work demonstrations, and special seasonal events. Among these is the Museum's popular quilt exhibition, an annual event held in June, which features both traditional and contemporary quilts.

The Mission Houses Museum welcomes the opportunity to participate in this distinguished exhibition of Hawaiian quilts and to share its collections with a new and appreciative audience. The Museum hopes that the people of Japan enjoy not only the fine workmanship of these Hawaiian quilts but what the quilts say about the lives of the women who made them, so that once again the quilts themselves might serve as a means of cultural understanding.

Deborah A. Pope
Mission Houses Museum

ドーターズオブハワイ

　ドーターズオブハワイ（ハワイの娘たち）は、アメリカプロテスタント宣教師の7人の娘たちによって滅びつつあるハワイの文化を保存しようと1903年に設立された。古きハワイを記録し、その精神を伝え、ハワイの言語の正しい発音、命名法を保持するというのが創立者たちの目的であった。会員は現在1400人ほどで、人種の差別はなく、1880年以前にハワイに居住したものの子孫であればだれでも入会することができる。ドーターズオブハワイは非営利団体であり、ボランティアの奉仕によって運営されている。ホノルルのクイーンエマ・サマーパレスとハワイ島のカイルア・コナにあるフリヘエパレスの2ヵ所に資料館を持ち、ハワイアンキルトをほとんど常時展示している。

キャサリーン・ソーン
ドーターズオブハワイ代表

Daughters of Hawai'i

　The Daughters of Hawai'i was founded in 1903 by seven women, daughters of American Protestant missionaries, who were keenly interested in the preservation of the Hawaiian culture which they felt might be lost forever. The founders of the organization wished to perpetuate the memory and spirit of old Hawai'i, and to preserve the nomenclature and correct pronunciation of the Hawaiian language. Membership, presently about 1,400, is open, with no racial restriction, to any woman who is directly descended from a person who lived in Hawai'i prior to 1880. The society is a non-profit corporation managed by a volunteer board of trustees.

　The Daughters of Hawai'i maintain and operate two historic sites as house museums, the Queen Emma Summer Palace in Honolulu and the Hulihe'e Palace in Kailua-Kona on the island of Hawai'i. Museum admission fees, donations, and membership dues form the bulk of the income to operate the two museums.

Catherine Thoene
Daughters of Hawai'i

Antique Quilts

Honolulu Academy of Arts

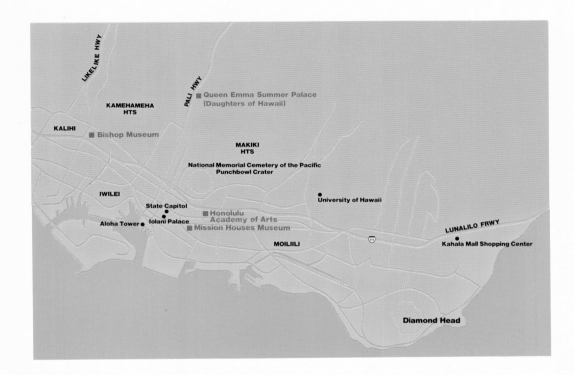

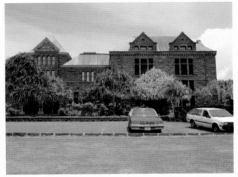

Bishop Museum

Mission Houses Museum

**Queen Emma Summer Palace
(Daughters of Hawai'i)**

1. クウハエアロハ　わがいとしの旗

作者不明
オアフ島
19世紀末〜20世紀初頭
ホノルル美術館蔵

　ハワイの旗のキルトは、そのほとんどが4枚の旗でキルトの周囲をかこみ、中心にハワイ王朝の紋章を入れている。このキルトもその例にもれない。ハワイの旗はカメハメハ大王の時代に初めてデザイン、使用された。大王と親交のあった英国の国旗ユニオンジャックを左端上におき、残りの部分にハワイ8島を象徴する8本の横縞を上から白、赤、青の順でくり返している。中心の紋章は、王朝初期には羽のケープを背景に、盾と王冠、その横にカメハメハ大王時代の2戦士・カマナワ、カメエイアモクが向き合って立つというデザインであった。カラカウア王の時代にこの紋章のデザインが複雑化し、新たに十字架が冠の上につけられ、第2の冠もケープの上に加えられ、2戦士は背中合わせに外側の方を向いて立つようになった。この作品はカラカウア王の要請で、王の友人であり、また政治顧問であったアレキサンダー・ウィリアム氏のために作られたもので、カラカウア時代の紋章のディテールがよく表されている。

KU'U HAE ALOHA
(My Beloved Flag)

Maker unknown
Island of O'ahu, late 19th century
Plain woven cotton, machine piecing, hand
**　applique, and straight and diamond**
**　quilting**
86″ (218cm.) × 84″ (213cm.)
Gift of Mrs. William P. Alexander, 1984
Honolulu Academy of Arts (#5217.1)

　This delightful and elaborate flag quilt is believed to have been commissioned by King Kalākaua for his friend and advisor William De Witt Alexander (1833-1913), a member of Kalākaua's privy council, a distinguished geographer and historian, and Surveyor-General of the Territory of Hawai'i for 30 years. This particular quilt was handed down over generations by family members as an heirloom.

　The quilt depicts four Hawaiian flags with Hawai'i's Coat of Arms at the center, the most common design used for Hawaiian flag quilts. The Hawaiian flag was first designed prior to 1816 for King Kamehameha I. It was taken down twice in history: at the time of brief British rule in 1843 and when the Kingdom was annexed to the United States in 1898. Many of the flag quilts are believed to have been made after the latter date, to symbolically preserve the glory of the Hawaiian Kingdom. The flag consists of eight stripes representing the eight major islands of Hawai'i and the Union Jack symbolizing the king's close association with Great Britain. The Hawai'i Coat of Arms was adopted in 1845. Originally its center shield was divided into four quarters, as depicted in this quilt, with stripes of the national banner in the first and third quarters and taboo ball and stick (pūlo'ulo'u) in the second and fourth. The small center escutcheon bore the triangular flag of the Hawaiian chief on two crossed spears. Both taboo ball and the flag-on-spears indicated protection and a place of refuge. Above the shield was a crown flanked by two warrior chiefs standing in feather cloak and helmet: Kamanawa holding a spear at the left and Kame'eiamoku, carrying a feather standard (kāhili) at the right, both facing inward. Later during King Kalākaua's reign, several changes occurred in the design. The Coat of Arms on this quilt depicts such later additions — the Maltese cross over the crown, a cross below the shield, and above it, a large second crown topped by another cross. The two chiefs stand facing outward rather than in the classic facing-inward stance.

ハワイ王朝の紋章　1885年頃
Hawaiian Coat of Arms c.1885
(Photograph courtesy of
Bishop Museum)

2. クウハエアロハ　わがいとしの旗

作者不明
ハワイ諸島
19世紀末〜20世紀初頭
ホノルル美術館蔵

　ここでは斜めに交差する小さい2本の旗が4組という慣例を破っためずらしい配置である。中心の紋章は線を強調してシンプルに、冠とケープは小さく上方にあしらわれ、2人の戦士はここでは除外されて、そのかわりシダの葉がスペースをうめている。キルティングはコントア（輪郭）キルティングでなく、めずらしく直線交差のダイアモンド形で、これが面白い効果をあげている。

KU'U HAE ALOHA
(My Beloved Flag)

Maker unknown
Hawaiian Islands, late 19th century to early
　20th century
Plain woven cotton, hand piecing, hand
　applique and diamond quilting
90.5″ (229.9cm.) × 84.5″ (214.6cm.)
Gift of Mrs. Levi Lawrence, 1956
Honolulu Academy of Arts (#2249.1)

　On this unusual flag quilt, eight small-sized Hawaiian flags, rather than the usual domineering four, fly on crossed poles against a spacious white background. The Coat of Arms at the center is delicately and beautifully designed in a linear style. King Kalākaua's cape and crown (see #5217.1) are diminished in size and here merely add a decorative touch to the crown on top of the oval shield. A fern-like plant growing from the bottom fills the space on both, usually occupied by two Hawaiian chiefs (trailing maidenhair fern was added to the Coat of Arms in the design of the Seal of the Provisional Government after 1893). The white ground is painstakingly quilted, not in the usual Hawaiian contour quilting, but in systematic "diamond in diamond" patterns which successfully reinforce the striking visual effect of this superb quilt.

3. クウハエアロハ わがいとしの旗

作者不明

ハワイ島

20世紀初頭

ホノルル美術館蔵

　ハワイの旗のキルトは旗と紋章という定まったデザイン要素で作られているので、一見みな同じような印象を受けるが、よく観察するとそのひとつひとつが作者の好みを反映してずいぶん違う。このカラカウア時代の紋章をデザインしたキルトは旗の縞が定例の8本でなく10本になっている。紋章の〝2人の戦士〟もここでは姿を消し、王冠はひとつだけで紺の地をバックにシンプルな形でまとまっている。

KU'U HAE ALOHA
(My Beloved Flag)

Maker unknown
Waimea, Island of Hawai'i, early 20th
**　century**
Plain woven cotton, hand piecing, hand
**　applique, and diagonal and contour**
**　quilting**
90″ (228.6cm.) × 90.5″ (229.9cm.)
Gift of Mrs. Richard M. Cooke, 1927
Honolulu Academy of Arts (#2590)

　The Royal Hawaiian Flag quilt is poignant in its expression of the quilter's nostalgia for the lost Hawaiian Kingdom. Flag quilts usually are considered sacred and are handed down as heirlooms. In most cases, they were never put to use, therefore, many remain in absolute mint condition. This beautiful quilt is an excellent example.

　The design of flag quilts, though generally following a standard pattern based on the Hawaiian flag and Coat of Arms, definitely expresses each quilter's individual taste in motifs, in colors, and in composition. Here, the quilter uses the familiar arrangement, four Hawaiian flags surrounding the central Coat of Arms. The flags, however, have ten stripes rather than the usual eight (representing Hawai'i's eight major islands). The Coat of Arms is well-designed. The large crown and ermine cape above are in the style adopted by King Kalākaua. The central shield has the familiar stripes, taboo balls, and sticks, but the two standing Hawaiian chiefs (depicted in #5217.1) are omitted from the design.

4. クウハエアロハ わがいとしの旗

作者不明
ハワイ諸島
19世紀末〜20世紀初頭
ホノルル美術館蔵

　このやや小さめの旗のキルトは、カリフォルニアのパサデナ劇場の舞台裏で発見された。どのような経過でこのキルトが劇場で使われるようになったかは不明である。キルト中央の紋章はカラカウア王時代のものであるが、その両側にめずらしく4つずつ白い8つの星がアップリケされている。これはハワイ8島を代表するものと思われる。星がハワイの紋章に初めて使用されたのは1893年から96年頃までの仮政府のときであった。

KU'U HAE ALOHA
(My Beloved Flag)

Maker unknown
Hawaiian Islands, late 19th century to early
　20th century
Plain woven cotton, hand piecing, hand
　applique, straight and contour quilting
74.5″ (189cm.) × 79″ (200.7cm.)
Gift of Mrs. Helmuth W. Hormann, 1989
Honolulu Academy of Arts (#5783.1)

　This lovely flag quilt, smaller than usual, was once used as a stage property at the Pasadena Playhouse in California. The familiar arrangement of four Hawaiian flags with eight stripes surrounds a central Hawaiian Coat of Arms surmounted by King Kalākaua's ermine cape and crown. The two warrior chiefs are, however, absent from this Coat of Arms (see #5217.1).

　Four stars on the two sides of the center design probably symbolize the eight major Hawaiian islands. The stars were first used in the Hawaiian Coat of Arms of the Seal of the Provisional Government formed after Queen Lili'uokalani was deposed and the monarchy overthrown in 1893 (the seal continued in use as late as 1896). In this seal, eight stars appear in the first and third quarters of the shield replacing the taboo sticks.

5. クウハエハワイ　私のハワイの旗

作者不明
カウアイ島
1900～1910年頃
ビショップ博物館蔵

　"クウハエハワイ"という文字がアップリケされた下にカラカウア王時代の紋章が細部まで大変忠実に表現されている。2つの王冠、そして外側を向いて背中合わせに立つカメハメハ大王当時の2人の戦士などが特徴である。この紋章をかこむハワイの旗は8本の横縞が入るがこれはハワイの主な8つの島・北からカウアイ、ニイハウ、オアフ、マウイ、ラナイ、カホオラウエ、ハワイの島々を表している。初期の旗の縞数はハワイ王朝の勢力範囲を象徴して7本、8本、9本の時もあったが1896年以後は8本と定められた。縞の色は上から白、赤、青のくり返しだが白は純潔、赤は血、すなわち生命を表し、青は継続つまりハワイ王朝の繁栄を願うものである。

カラカウア王　1882～1891年頃
King Kalākaua, c. 1882-1891. (Photograph courtesy of Bishop Museum)

KU'U HAE HAWAI'I
(My Hawaiian Flag or My Flag of Hawai'i)

Maker unknown
Island of Kaua'i, circa 1900-1910
Plain woven cotton, machine stitching, hand applique, contour and diagonal quilting
84″ (214cm.) × 84″ (214cm.)
Gift of Augusta Suder, 1970
Bernice Pauahi Bishop Museum (#1970.53)

　The fabric used in this piece came from England and the quilt was given to Augusta Suder by Miss Lucy Wilcox around 1940.

　The Coat of Arms shown is that of the Kalākaua period and includes the representation of the twins, Kame'eiamoku and Kamanawa, two among five chiefs who supported Kamehameha I as their leader.

　Prior to 1896, the Hawaiian flag contained as few as seven stripes or as many as nine stripes. Since 1896, there have been eight stripes representing the major islands in an order of north to south, from top to bottom: Kaua'i, Ni'ihau, O'ahu, Molokai, Maui, Lāna'i, Kaho'olawe, and Hawai'i. Each color of the stripes is symbolic: white for purity, placed at the top; red for blood which is life; and blue for continuity — the Kingdom will endure.

　The stitching of the applique is a catch stitch, a technique used when the edges of the applique were not turned under.

6. クウハエアロハ　わがいとしの旗

作者不明
オアフ島
19世紀末〜20世紀初頭
ビショップ博物館蔵

　一見同じようにみえる旗のキルトも紋章のデザイン、旗の組み合わせ方は千差万別である。この作品の旗はユニオンジャックと8本の縞の位置が入れかわって、ちょうど裏から見たような状態でデザインされている。旗の長い方の縞は、はぎ目がないが、途中で布が足りなくなったのであろうか、短い青い縞の部分は何枚かのつぎはぎパッチワークになっている。ユニオンジャックの赤と白の交差する線はミシンで縫い、それを手縫いでアップリケするというミシンと手縫いがまざった作品である。

KU'U HAE ALOHA
(My Beloved Flag)

Maker unknown
**Island of O'ahu, late 19th or early 20th
　　century**
**Plain woven cotton, machine stitching, hand
　　applique, and contour quilting**
69″ (175cm.) × 69″ (175cm.)
Gift of Norine Potter Kennedy, 1974
Bernice Pauahi Bishop Museum (# 1974.21)

This flag quilt is of the Kalākaua period, as indicated by the two crowns present in the Coat of Arms design. The creativity exhibited by the makers of flag quilts is evidenced by the variety of Coat of Arms designs found in the various flag quilts, as well as different ways of placing the flags around the center design. The most traditional flag placement is considered to be when the flag's union jack is placed under the left bottom corner of the central design and the stripes extend to the border of the quilt. The rest of the flags would then continue in a like manner counter clock-wise around the quilt. In this quilt, the flags are placed backwards.

The shorter blue stripes in the flags of this quilt have been pieced, whereas the rest of the stripes are made from a single piece of fabric. The union jacks are machine sewn and then hand appliqued to the quilt.

7. ハワイのフラッグキルト

作者不明
ハワイ諸島
19世紀末〜20世紀初頭
ビショップ博物館蔵

　この作品は通常のキルトよりずっと小さい。むしろ壁かけのサイズといってよく、旗のモチーフの扱い方も独特で作者の〝ステートメント〟ともいうべき特殊な作品である。旗は前ページのキルトと同じくユニオンジャックが右端にくる裏返しの状態で、縞の数も上下の2枚が10本ずつ、左右が7本ずつと、これも大変変わっている。使用されたことがないためか、保存状態は非常に良く、裏にインクでソロモン・カハレアというサインが入っている。このキルトを贈られた人の名であろうと思われる。

HAWAIIAN FLAG QUILT

Maker unknown
Hawaiian Islands, late 19th to early 20th
　century
Plain woven cotton, machine piecing, hand
　applique, contour and straight quilting
68.5″ (174cm.) × 53″ (135cm.)
On loan from Mrs. Harriet Dillingham, 1989
Bernice Pauahi Bishop Museum
　(TL #1989.41)

　This small flag quilt from the Kalākaua period was probably not meant to be a bed cover but was made as a statement piece. This would explain the idiosyncracies in some of the pattern elements such as the number of stripes and the flag placement.

　Very little is known about the history of this quilt. The owner recalls that it was given to her family in the 1930s or 1940s. The quilt is in excellent condition and the name Solomon Kahalewa is written in ink on a back corner. It is not known what the relationship of the quilt to this individual was, although it is possible the quilt was made for him.

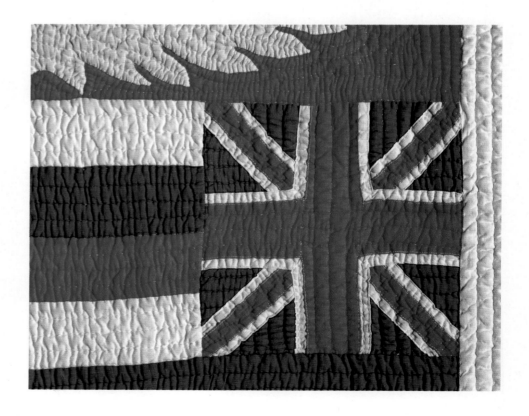

33

8. クウハエアロハ わがいとしの旗

ウィルヘルミナ・アイシンガーとエノス夫人
マウイ島
1918年頃
ビショップ博物館蔵

マウイ島のワイルク地方で乳製業を営んでいたピーター・アイシンガーの夫人ウィルヘルミナがハワイ原住のエノス夫人と共同で制作したキルトといわれる。艶のあるコットンを使い、色も淡いピンクで他の旗のキルトとは全く違う特徴を出している。刺繍の技術はすばらしく、クウハエアロハという字、また紋章内の盾、ケープなどにあざやかな黄色の刺繍がなされていて、それが作品の美しいアクセントになっている。紋章のある中心部はコントアキルティングで旗の部分は斜めに交差する直線のキルティングで変化をつけている。かすかな鉛筆のガイドラインがまだ布地に残っている。

KU'U HAE ALOHA
(My Beloved Flag)

Wilhelmina Eichinger and Mrs. Enos, makers
Island of Maui, circa 1918
Twill woven polished (sateen) cotton,
machine piecing, hand applique and
embroidery, contour and diagonal
quilting
84.1″ (214cm.) × 84″ (213cm.)
Gift of J. Stanley and Charles Robert
Eichinger, 1984
Bernice Pauahi Bishop Museum
(#1984.371.01)

Mrs. Eichinger, who arrived in Hawai'i in 1914, and Mrs. Enos, a Hawaiian woman, made this quilt circa 1918 in Wailuku, Maui. Mrs. Eichinger's husband, Peter Walter Eichinger, was the builder of the Pu'unēnē and Waihe'e dairies in Maui.

The unusual color of this flag quilt appears to be the original coloring and is not the result of aging or fading. The polished cotton fabric certainly adds to this quilt's distinction. The embroidery work and detailing are exceptional. Contour quilting is used on the central Coat of Arms and diagonal quilting is used on the flag elements. The diagonals are spaced 3″ and 1.5″ apart, creating a design within a design. The embroidery work on the words and along the edge of the upper banner accentuates the Coat of Arms. The two crowns indicate that the Coat of Arms is of the Kalākaua period. Faint pencil lines are visible on the quilt but do not detract from its overall beauty.

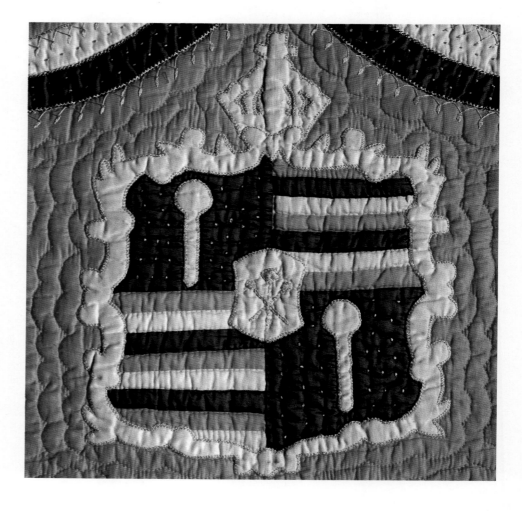

35

9. タイトル不明

作者不明
ハワイ島
1906年
ミッションハウス博物館蔵

　この作品は紋章のかわりに初期の旗の
キルトのデザインによくみられる単一王
冠と〝マモ〟のレイを組み合わせたもの
を中心においている。4枚の旗は上下左
右が対称になるような位置で組み合わさ
れ、ユニオンジャックは小さく、キルト
の4辺に接しておかれている。縞の順序
も正しい白、赤、青でなく、それをひっ
くり返した青、赤、白となっている。〝マ
モ〟のレイを王冠のまわりに使っている
のは、小さい黄色い〝マモ〟の花が王族
のケープその他に使われた同じく〝マモ〟
と呼ばれる貴重な鳥の羽に似ているとこ
ろから、王族のシンボルとして使われた
という慣例によったものと思われる。〝マ
モ〟のまわりのキルティングが花びらの
ように美しい。

QUILT NAME UNKNOWN

Maker unknown
Island of Hawai'i, 1906
Plain woven cotton, wool batting, hand and
　machine piecing, hand applique, contour
　and straight quilting
86″ (218cm.) × 88″ (223.5cm.)
Gift of Doreen Bicknell Griep, 1982
Mission Houses Museum (#82.4.1.B8)

　This quilt was made as a wedding gift for
James and Aimee Gribble Bicknell in 1906. It
may have been made, as were other family
quilts, by women at Hāwī, North Kohala, on
the Island of Hawai'i where James Bicknell
(1869-1962) grew up. The flag quilt design
may have been chosen because Mr. Bicknell
was the County Auditor. He later became the
first auditor for the City and County of
Honolulu, a position he held for 27 years.
　The central motif of this Hawaiian flag
quilt draws on an earlier design tradition in
which the *mamo* lei together with the single
crown of the 1845 royal Coat of Arms was
used. The flags are placed to mirror each
other. The maker also chose to rearrange the
sequence of colored stripes so that the top
flag is different from the others. The lei is cut
open rather than in the traditional eight-fold
pattern.
　The leaves of the *mamo*, or false saffron
flower (*Carthamus tinctorius)* also have been
used to evoke the symbol of royalty. The
small yellow flowers resemble the yellow
feather leis worn by royalty (*ali'i*). The gold-
en yellow feathers were plucked from above
and beneath the black tail feathers and from
the thighs of the black *mamo* bird (*Drepanis
pacifica*), a species that lived only on the island of Hawai'i, home of Kamehameha the
Great. A feather cape made solely of the
scarce *mamo* feathers was worn only by the
king of an island as his battle cloak.

10. ハワイのフラッグキルト

旧ミッション教会の女性たちの共作

オアフ島

1910年頃

ミッションハウス博物館蔵

　このキルトはハワイ統治領時代の判事であったローリン・アンドリュース三世のために教会の女性たちが共同で制作したもの。ここでも旗のユニオンジャックが反対側につけられ縞数は６本だけという独自のものになっている。中央の紋章は紅を地に華やかな黄色で力強くデザインされて、紅と黄というハワイ王朝好みの色調がよく表されている。ケープが大変小さく、そのかわりシダの葉が大きく下からささえるようにのびている。これはカラカウア王の紋章の変型であるが、初めてこの複雑なカラカウア紋が記録されたのは1883年。王の即位式の招待状に使われた時であった。

HAWAIIAN FLAG QUILT

Made by the women of the old Mission Church
Island of O'ahu, circa 1910
Plain woven cotton, wool batting, machine piecing, hand applique, contour and straight quilting
85″ (215.9cm.) × 77.7″ (196.9cm.)
Gift of Mrs. Leslie L. Fulton, 1971
Mission Houses Museum (#71.45.A2)

This quilt was made for Lorrin Andrews, II "...by the women of the old Mission Church about 1910." The Hawaiian flag quilt pattern may well have been chosen to commemorate the family's historic ties with the government of Hawai'i as well as with the old Mission Church (probably Kawaiaha'o Church in Honolulu). At the time this quilt was made, Mr. Andrews already had served as the Attorney General of the Territory of Hawai'i. His grandfather, the Reverend Lorrin Andrews (1795-1868), came to Hawai'i as a missionary and founded the Lahainaluna Seminary for Hawaiian students on Maui in 1831. He was appointed under King Kamehameha III to serve as Judge of the Court of O'ahu in Honolulu in 1845. He later became the first Associate Justice of Hawai'i's Supreme Court.

It was also in 1845 that the first royal Coat of Arms was adopted for use by the Hawaiian Kingdom and a new flag, with eight stripes representing the eight major islands, was unfurled. This quilt is unusual in that there are only six stripes in each flag, and the order of color has been changed. The central motif is based on the later, more ornate double-crowned Coat of Arms which first appeared on the invitations to the coronation of King Kalākaua in 1883.

39

11. ハワイのフラッグキルト

作者不明

ハワイ諸島

1905年頃

ドーターズオブハワイ資料館蔵

　中心の少々変わった紋章は1843年英国でカメハメハ三世のためにデザインされ、三世の紋として使われたものをモデルにしている。2人の戦士の足元をつなぐようにカメハメハ王朝のモットーである「国土の生命は正義の内に守られる」という言葉が刺繍されている。旗の部分はこの作者の遊びであろうか、ユニオンジャックの位置が変わり、縞は長短があって矩形の旗というイメージはくずされている。アップリケの布地は切り端を折り込まず、そのまま見せてその上をキャッチステッチ（千鳥がけ）でおさえているのも変わっている。

HAWAIIAN FLAG QUILT

Maker unknown
Hawaiian Islands, circa 1905
Plain woven cotton, hand and machine
　applique, diagonal and diamond quilting
79.5″ (201.9cm.) × 77″ (183cm.)
Gift of Mrs. William H. Shipman, 1928
Daughters of Hawai'i (# 1196),
　　Queen Emma Summer Palace

There are several aspects of this Hawaiian flag quilt that are noteworthy. The center Coat of Arms is of a design prior to the changes made by King Kalākaua around 1883. The Coat of Arms for the Kingdom was created during the reign of King Kamehameha Ⅲ and was produced by the College of Arms in England around 1843. The motto of the Kingdom as it appears under the coat of arms is *Ua mau Ka ea o ‥ i ka pono,* and translates as ''The Life of the Land is Perpetuated in Righteousness,'' a phrase attributed to Kamehameha Ⅲ when the British briefly ruled the Kingdom in 1843. The third word, ''ka'' (the), was later changed to ''ke'' (the) probably for euphonic reasons.

The union jacks of the flags are not placed in the usual manner for a flag quilt, and the result is not a true flag representation as is evidenced by the four short stripes and the four long ones on each flag. The stem-stitch embroidery work in the center is quite remarkable and unique. The single thread catch-stitch used for the applique work indicates the raw edges of the applique fabric were not turned under.

40

41

12. ハワイのフラッグキルト

作者不明
ハワイ諸島
19世紀末
ドーターズオブハワイ資料館蔵

　大きな4つの星が中心部の四隅にあしらわれているが、これは作者の先祖がアメリカ独立戦争に参加したことを記念したのではないかといわれている。中央の紋章はカラカウア王以前のものをモデルにしている。アップリケの糸は1インチに24目と非常に細かい。ユニオンジャックと盾内部の白い線を表すのに洋服の裾回りにつけるバイヤステープがそのまま使われている。このテープは1800年末から1900年初頭にかけて便利であったせいか、たびたびキルトに利用されており、作品の年代を知るひとつの手がかりとして貴重なものである。

HAWAIIAN FLAG QUILT

Maker unknown
Hawaiian Islands, late 19th century
Plain woven cotton, machine piecing, hand applique and contour and straight quilting
82″ (208cm.) × 83″ (210cm.)
Gift of Mr. and Mrs. C. Wilbur Craw, 1982
Daughters of Hawai'i (#2622),
**　　Queen Emma Summer Palace**

　The unique inclusion of four large stars in the corners of the center area of this quilt expresses the quilt maker's pride in an ancestor's participation in America's War of Independence (1775-1783). The crest is taken from a design established prior to King Kalākaua's rule.

　The overcast applique stitching in the center is an incredible 24 stitches to the inch. The quilting treatment inside the stripes of the flag is quite unusual, and penciled guidelines are visible on the stripes. Hemming tape is used in the union jacks of the flags and the center of the crest, a frequent occurrence in flag quilts made in the late 1800s and early 1900s. The binding around the quilt's perimeter is made by bringing the backing fabric to the front and top-stitching it by machine.

43

13. アメリカのフラッグキルト

作者不明

制作地不明

1907～1910年頃

ドーターズオブハワイ資料館蔵

　ハワイの旗のキルトの様式をそのまま
使った作品であるが、扱っているテーマ
はアメリカのものである。オクラホマ州
が46番目の州として1907年に合衆国に仲
間入りをしたが、このキルトの旗は46の
星を持ち、その当時の作品と思われる。
紋章の中で羽を広げたブルーの鷲が口に
くわえているのは「多数の融合」という
合衆国のモットーを刺繍した旗である。
アメリカの色・赤、白、青があざやかで
星条旗のマーチが聞こえてきそうな作品
である。

AMERICAN FLAG QUILT

Maker unknown
Location unknown, circa 1907-1910
Plain woven cotton, machine piecing, hand
**   applique, contour and straight quilting**
84″ (213cm.) × 83.75″ (212cm.)
Gift of Marjorie Manoheali'i Booth Stephens,
**   1969**
Daughters of Hawai'i (#916.102),
**   Queen Emma Summer Palace**

Although the subject matter of this quilt is
American, the design and construction are in
the manner of the Hawaiian flag quilts: four
flags surrounding a central Coat of Arms or
crest. Here we find four American flags, circa
1907-1910, surrounding a modification of the
Great Seal of America. The 46 stars in the
flag represent the states in the Union at that
time. Oklahoma became the 46th state in
1907; New Mexico and Arizona became the
47th and 48th states in 1910.

The center design is a modification of the
Great Seal of America. The banner held by
the eagle contains the motto ''E Pluribus
Unum'' (Out of Many One). The chain stitch
is used for the motto as well as the yellow embroidery on the eagle. The applique stitch for
the center pieces and the stars in the flags is
a catch stitch indicating the raw edges of the
fabric were not turned under.

45

14. 王冠とカヒリ

メアリー・S・ライスの作と伝えられる
カウアイ島
1886年頃
ホノルル美術館蔵

鳥の羽で作った〝カヒリ〟と呼ばれる王族用の飾り物は手に持つ小さなものから、台つきの頭上高くそびえる大きなものまで各種いろいろ存在する。ハワイ王朝の重要な行事には王族のシンボルとして〝カヒリ〟が必ず登場する。赤い羽で作った〝カヒリ〟が最も多いのに比して〝オオ〟と呼ばれる黒いミツスイ科の鳥の尾からとったカヒリは数が少なく大変珍重された。このキルトはその〝カヒリ〟をテーマにこれを王冠と組み合わせ、白地に紅というクラシックな配色で力強く、見事にまとめている。作者は19世紀後半ハワイで伝道につとめた宣教師ウィリアム・ハリソン・ライスの妻メアリー・ライスと伝えられる。メアリーは教会で、また学校でたくさんの子供たちを教え、その暖かい性格から子供たちに〝マザーライス〟と呼ばれ慕われた。キルトの裏にメアリー・ソフィア・ライス1886年というインクのサインがある。

マザーライス
Mother Rice (Mrs. William Harrison Rice), date unknown. (Photograph courtesy of Mission Houses Museum)

NA KALAUNU ME NA KĀHILI
(Crowns and Kāhili)

Attributed to Mary Sophia Rice
Island of Kaua'i, circa 1886
Plain woven cotton, hand applique, and
  contour quilting
75″ (190.5cm.) × 75″ (190.5cm.)
Gift of Mrs. Thomas D. King, Jr., 1973
Honolulu Academy of Arts (#4182.1)

The *kāhili* was a feather standard, a symbol of royalty and an insignia of the highest rank in the Kingdom of Hawai'i. Large *kāhili* were used on official state occasions and after each use the *kāhili* were carefully dismantled in order to preserve the valuable feathers. Feathers of many kinds of birds were used to make *kāhili*. Used in only the most sacred *kāhili* were the feathers of the '*ō'ō* (several endemic species of black honeyeaters, genus *Acrulocercus*), while the brilliant red feathers of the honeycreeper '*i'iwi* (*Vestiaria coccinea*) were used in abundance for *kāhili* of all sizes. This royal symbol often was depicted in Hawaiian quilt designs.

This stunning quilt, though small in size, is adorned with striking multiple images of *kāhili* Four large feather standards in classic turkey red radiate boldly from the center against a white background, powerfully surrounding and protecting four royal crowns. The curves of the *kāhili* are echoed by carefully contoured quilting.

The quilt is attributed to Mary Sophia Rice, a native of New York, either as quilter or designer, as an inscription on the back reads ''M.S. Rice, Kahili, 1886.'' Married to missionary William Harrison Rice (1816-1911), she arrived in Honolulu with her husband in 1840. After being stationed in Hāna and Lahaina on the Island of Maui, the couple came to Honolulu where she served as matron of Punahou School. She was greatly loved by the children she taught for her warm and sincere personality and was widely known as Mother Rice.

47

15. 王　冠

作者不明

ハワイ諸島

20世紀初頭

ホノルル美術館蔵

　ハワイのキルトとしてはめずらしい中間色を使った作品。淡い藤色と柔らかい黄色が落ち着いたムードを作り出している。テーマは王冠とシダの葉、その中に〝カヒリ〟と思われるモチーフがアレンジされている。このような王族にちなんだモチーフを持つキルトには旗のキルト同様、滅びてしまった昔日のハワイ王朝を偲ぶハワイの人たちの思いが込められている。

カピオラニ女王の冠
Queen Kapiʻolani's crown. (Photograph courtesy of Bishop Museum)

NA KALAUNU (Crown)

Maker unknown
Hawaiian Islands, early 20th century
Plain woven cotton, hand applique, contour
quilting, and machine edging
82.5″ (209.5cm.) × 81.5″ (207cm.)
Gift of Mrs. C.M. Cooke Estate, 1938
Honolulu Academy of Arts (#4703)

This lovely quilt is made in an unusual color combination of pale lavender and soft yellow, a departure from the usual combination of solid bright red or blue on a stark white ground. Turkey red and white have been considered the classic colors of Hawaiian quilts, perhaps because fabric dyed in red was easily available in the 19th century and traditional Hawaiian red and white *kapa* designs were already there to inspire quilters. In the course of time, many different colors appeared on quilters' palettes, suiting the subjects and moods of their designs. Interestingly, almost no printed fabric was used by Hawaiian quilters, nor were combinations of several colors tried, as is common in mainland American quilting. Typically in Hawaiian quilts, as in this example, only two colors interact to produce a dynamic design. Here the unidentified central design, possibly suggesting four *kāhili* or feather standards, is surrounded by eight ferns and eight crowns (*kalaunu*). The design may have been intended to express aloha toward the *aliʻi* (royalty) and the Hawaiian Kingdom.

16. カイウラニの櫛

作者不明
ハワイ島
20世紀初頭
ホノルル美術館蔵

　プリンセス・カイウラニは1875年ハワイ王朝のたそがれの時代に知事アーチボルド・スコット・クレグホーンとプリンセス・リケリケとの間に生まれた。カラカウア王とその妹で、ハワイ王朝の最後の女王であるリリウオカラニは母方の伯父、伯母にあたる。このリリウオカラニ女王が退位を余儀なくされた時、唯一の後継者であったカイウラニはハワイ王国再建の希望を首都ワシントンに赴き、一心になって陳情したが成功しなかった。スポーツにすぐれ、容姿たおやかで人気があったが、1899年24才の短い生涯を終えた。このキルトはその薄幸ともいうべきカイウラニ王女に捧げたもので、カイウラニの使用した櫛とレイを主題にそれにハワイ8島を象徴する8つの星を周囲にあしらっている。キルティングは面白いことに手縫いでなく、ミシンでなされている。ミシンの使用は19世紀の半ば頃からハワイでも始まったと思われ、この作品はたぶん新しい文明の利器を自慢したかったのかもしれない。

プリンセス カイウラニ 1889～1897年頃
Princess Ka'iulani, c.1889-1897. (Photograph courtesy of Bishop Museum)

KE KAHI O KA'IULANI
(The Comb of Ka'iulani)

Maker Unknown
Island of Hawai'i, early 20th century
Plain woven cotton, hand applique, and
**　　machine quilting**
88.5″ (224.8cm.) × 84″ (213.4cm.)
Gift of Mrs. Richard A. Cooke, 1927
Honolulu Academy of Arts (#2591)

Hawaiian quilt designs often reflect the makers' aloha for and adoration of their beloved monarchs. This marvelous quilt commemorates Princess Ka'iulani (1875-1899) who lived in the twilight years of the Hawaiian Kingdom. Ka'iulani was the daughter of Governor Archibald Scott Cleghorn and Princess Likelike, and niece of the last two reigning monarchs of Hawai'i, King Kalākaua and Queen Lili'uokalani. The princess often was portrayed as the last hope of the Kingdom and in fact traveled to Washington, D.C., after the overthrow of the monarchy to plead for the restoration of the throne. Known for her beauty, she was widely loved for her many artistic and athletic talents. The pattern of this quilt commemorates the princess by depicting her hair combs decorated with crowns and leis of leaves all radiating from the center. The details of the combs and crowns are lovingly expressed in open-work designs. Two sets of eight stars in a square on the outer edges and in a circle within the main design, probably symbolize the eight major islands of Hawai'i. Quilting is executed, as on the grapevine quilt (#2589), by straight parallel machine stitching one inch apart in vertical and horizontal directions. It is possible that this quilt and the grapevine quilt were made by the same quilter from Waimea, Island of Hawai'i.

17. カイウラニの扇子と羽根飾り

メアリー・アン・K・P・ミュラー作
オアフ島
1917年頃
ビショップ博物館蔵

　前ページの "カイウラニの櫛" と同様、このキルトも薄幸のプリンセス・カイウラニに棒げた作品である。彼女の扇子と羽根飾り（カヒリ）がここでは大きく拡大されてキルト一杯に広がり、みるからに力強い作品になっている。キルティンググラインをマークした鉛筆のあとがまだ残っているほか、台または枠に固定してキルティングをしたと思われる布表面に片寄ったふくらみがところどころに見える。

カヒリ
A pair of hand *kāhili.* (Photograph courtesy of Bishop Museum).

FAN AND FEATHER PLUME OF KA'IULANI

Mary Ann Kekaula Palaualelo Muller, maker
Island of O'ahu, circa 1917
Twill woven cotton, hand applique, diagonal
**　　quilting, and machine edging**
83″ (210cm.) × 78″ (198cm.)
Gift of Helen Harue Kakumitsu Suder and
**　　Mr. Elston Kahiwahiwaakealoha Suder,**
**　　1984**
Bernice Pauahi Bishop Museum
**　　(#1984.364.001)**

　This striking quilt was made by Mary Ann Kekaula Palaualelo Muller for Elston Kahiwahiwaakealoha Suder at the time of his birth.

　The fan and feather plume is a popular design with Hawaiian quilters. In this example, the red twill was pieced and appliqued to the white background at 16 stitches per inch. Pencil lines mark the quilting rows on the bias of the quilt. The binding on the edge is the same fabric as the applique.

　When a quilt is placed on a quilting horse or large frame, the quilter sometimes will work on the area that is wrapped around the frame's pole. When removed from the frame, this area of quilting will appear slightly puckered when compared to the other areas of quilting. If the quilting frame is about twenty inches wide, these areas of puckering will appear every twenty inches. This quilt shows evidence of having been done on a frame.

18. タイトル不明

アニー・フェルプス作
オアフ島
1850年〜1860年頃
ビショップ博物館蔵

　このキルトの作者アニー・フェルプス
は子供時代ハワイ王朝最後の女王リリウ
オカラニの遊び友だちであったという。
後にさとうきび農場の技術者と結婚して
いる。この作品は彼女自身のデザインで
かわいい小さいいくつかのモチーフをそ
れぞれ独立させてアップリケし、色も赤、
青、緑の三色を使いわけている。手法と
してはアメリカ本土のキルトによく似て
いるが、中央の王冠のモチーフ、コント
アキルティングの使用など、やはりハワ
イアンキルトの伝統の中で生まれた作品
といってよいであろう。

QUILT NAME UNKNOWN

Annie Phelps, maker
Island of O'ahu, circa 1850-1860
Plain woven calico, machine and hand
** piecing, hand applique, and contour**
** quilting**
86″ (215cm.) × 86″ (215cm.)
Gift of Dorothy Bowman, 1984
Bernice Pauahi Bishop Museum
** (#1984.374.001)**

　This quilt was made by the donor's great
aunt, Annie Phelps, who according to family
stories, was a childhood friend of Queen
Lili'uokalani. The quilter's husband, Caspar
Phelps, came to Hawai'i from California in
the late 1850s as an engineer for one of
Hawai'i's sugar plantations. The design of
this quilt is Annie Phelp's own.

　This quilt uses a number of traditional
American techniques — the piecing of the
separate designs and the use of several colors.
However, the Hawaiian influence is evident
in the crown motif.

　The quilt is superbly appliqued and the
contour quilting pattern changes throughout
the quilt.

マーガレット・A・アハクエロ作
オアフ島
1930年頃
ミッションハウス博物館蔵

このキルトはカメハメハ大王の妃カア
フマヌに棒げたもの。カアフマヌはカメ
ハメハ大王に最も愛された妃で、大王の
よき相談相手であり、その死後はカメハ
メハ二世と共に政治に携わった。"カプ"
と呼ばれた古い宗教的な掟を排し、新し
い社会法律を確立制定させたことで知ら
れている。このキルトは1930年頃に作ら
れ、ちょうどカアフマヌ誕生100年にあた
り作者はそれを祝うつもりであったと思
われる。ハワイ王朝が好んで使ったあざ
やかな黄色で王冠、カヒリ、シダなどが
アップリケされている。テクニックは見
事で中央のサークルの中、カアフマヌの
名が通常のアップリケの手法でなくリバ
ース（裏返し）アップリケと呼ばれる、
切った布の間からその下の地の色をみせ
ていくやり方でなされている。

このキルトのモチーフであるカアフマヌ ソ
サイエテイのバッヂをつけた作者
Mrs. Ahakuelo (1891-1969) is wearing the
pin of the Ka'ahumanu Society, the
emblem of which forms the central medallion on her quilt. A practicioner of other
traditional Hawaiian arts, she also wove
the hat and feather lei.　　　(Photograph
courtesy of Mission Houses Museum)

QUILT NAME UNKNOWN

Margaret Apiki Ahakuelo, maker
Island of O'ahu, circa 1930
Plain woven cotton, wool batting, machine
** piecing, hand applique including reverse**
** applique, and contour quilting**
100.5″ (255.3cm.) × 93.5″ (237.49cm.)
Gift of Mrs. Margaret K. Fette, 1980
Mission Houses Museum (#80.9.1.NM)

This quilt of crowns and *kāhili* honors
Ka'ahumanu, the favorite wife of King
Kamehameha the Great. His companion and
confidante, she was also a great chiefess in
her own right. At his death in 1819, Ka'a-
humanu created for herself the role of *kuhina
nui*, or co-ruler, with the new king. She was
able to consolidate such strength and power
that the position of *kuhina nui* became the
central feature of governmental organization.
Under her direct influence, the old system of
religious law (*kapu*) was set aside, the beginnings of secular law were established, and
Christianity was accepted as the Kingdom's
new religion.

This lovely quilt is thought to have been
made in the 1930s. One wonders if the quilt
maker privately was observing the centenary
of Ka'ahumanu's death in 1833. The quality
of workmanship is very fine. There is great
constancy in the spacing of the quilting rows
and the placement of the stitches, six to the
inch. The center crown is cut in one piece and
Ka'ahumanu's name is worked in reverse
applique, while the border lei with the crown
and *kāhili* motifs is cut in the traditional
eight-fold method.

20. レフアの花にやさしく降る雨

作者不明

ハワイ諸島

19世紀末

ホノルル美術館蔵

　レフアの木はハワイ各地、海岸の低地から山の斜面にかけてどこにでもみられ、小さく繊細な花を一年中咲かせている。花はあざやかな紅と黄色があり、中心が長い細毛でおおわれているのが特徴である。ハワイの伝説では火山の女神ペレが愛した花として歌や物語に再三登場する。このキルトはそのレフアの花を黄色に、地色を赤にしデリケートなレフアの花と葉のまわりを〝コントアキルティング〟がうねうねと水輪のようにとりまいて、題名の〝やさしく降る雨〟というムードをよく出している。赤と黄という色合わせはハワイ王族が好んで使ったもので、このキルトも意識的にその配合を選んだと考えられる。

KA UA KANI LEHUA
(The Rain That Rustles Lehua Blossoms)

Maker unknown
Hawaiian Islands, late 19th century
Plain woven cotton, hand applique, and
**　contour quilting**
78″ (198.1cm.) × 84″ (213.4cm.)
Gift of Mr. Damon Gifford, 1959
Honolulu Academy of Arts (#2608.1)

Lehua is the flower of the *'ōhi'a* tree (*Metrosideros collina*), one of the most common plants found in Polynesia that grows from sea level to the mountains. The *lehua* is recognized by its bright scarlet (or sometimes yellow) clusters of flowers bearing numerous long stamens. According to Hawaiian legend, this delicate flower is sacred to Pele, goddess of fire and volcano, and a garland or lei made of *lehua* is said to be her favorite. The *lehua* flower is occasionally used as a motif on Hawaiian quilts.

　In this truly superb 19th-century example, delicate *lehua* blossoms decorate a red ground, now faded to brick-red. The lyrical title of the quilt, The Rain That Rustles the Lehua Blossoms, is well-expressed by intricate flower patterns and numerous fine contour lines of quilting which ripple like water around the flowers. The combination of red and yellow may be intended as a reference to the colors of the ancient Hawaiian feather capes and cloaks which were symbols of monarchy.

21. やさしくおさえて

作者不明
ハワイ諸島
19世紀末〜20世紀初頭
ホノルル美術館蔵

　ハワイのキルトの名前の中にはこの作品のように非常に抽象的な名がたびたび出てくる。全く作者個人の感情から出たものと思われる。この〝やさしくおさえて〟もそのリリカルなムードは共通性を持って見る者に呼びかける。紺と白という清潔な配合で植物のパターンがデリケートな線でちょうどレースのように中心から広がっている。中心のモチーフは櫛であるともいわれる。

KAOMI MĀLIE (Press Gently)

Maker unknown
Hawaiian Islands, late 19th century to early
　　20th century
Plain woven cotton, hand applique, and
　　contour quilting
79″ (200.7cm.) × 82″ (208cm.)
Gift of Mrs. Albert Wilcox, 1927
Honolulu Academy of Arts (#2272)

　The naming of a quilt design is always the originator's privilege. Although most Hawaiian quilts have been given straightforward and unambiguous names, some have poetic or symbolic, and indeed puzzling, names, entertaining viewers by encouraging their imaginations. While universal human feelings may be suggested by provocative motifs, a pattern may also express a particular emotion, mood, or idea. Sometimes Hawaiian quilters give their quilts wholly private names with hidden meanings known only to themselves. Here, an unidentified leaf design has been given the poetic, abstract name "Press Gently." The cool blue color of the leaves against the white background creates a serene and gentle mood. The pattern, spreading like a net from a center motif said to suggest combs, is delicately linear and has a feminine, lace-like quality. The quilt's four corners are adorned with equally delicate wreath-like patterns.

22. 虹の端

作者不明

ハワイ諸島

19世紀末〜20世紀初頭

ホノルル美術館蔵

　初期のキルトはそれぞれが作者の創る心を反映して独自のデザインが多かった。他人のパターンを無断で借用することは原則としてタブーであったが、それでも非常にすぐれたデザインにはその後何度もほかのキルターたちによって使われてきた。作者の承諾を得た場合も、無断の場合もあったであろうと思われる。他人のパターンを借りた場合、新しい名前をつけることによってそこに新しい意味が生まれ、パターンを多少違えることによってデザインに変化が加えられた。この作品は〝虹の端〟と名づけられているが、もともとは〝マウイの美〟と呼ばれたキルトの変型である。ハワイの虹は雨あがりにさんさんたる太陽の光を反射して見事に大きく山上に出現する。作品の四辺の半円型のくり返しはその虹のイメージをとらえようとしたのかもしれない。

LIHILIHI ĀNUENUE
(Edge of the Rainbow)

Maker unknown
Hawaiian Islands, late 19th century to early
　20th century
Plain woven cotton, hand applique, and
　contour quilting
89″ (223.5cm.) × 87″ (221.0cm.)
Gift of Mrs. Charles M. Cooke Estate, 1938
Honolulu Academy of Arts (#4702)

　From the beginning of Hawaiian quilting, numerous one-of-a-kind designs have been conceived by the creative minds of their makers. Each quilter's patterns were indeed their personal expressions and in the old days, they were considered the exclusive property of their creators. It was taboo to steal another's designs. Yet, it was also common that a beautiful pattern would become popular perhaps because quilters shared the same sentiment. The quilt might be copied, either with permission of the originator, or altered to make the design slightly different from the original. A new name often was given to a variation by its maker or, in some cases, by the quilt's owner. The pattern of this particular quilt, titled Edge of the Rainbow, is a variation of the design commonly known as Maui Beauty (see Introduction, p.14), suggesting the quilt originated on the Island of Maui. An intricate flower-like center motif is well-balanced by an equally delicate border design, the arc-shaped lines of which bring to mind the numerous beautiful rainbows that are caused by the mingling rain and sun in Hawai'i.

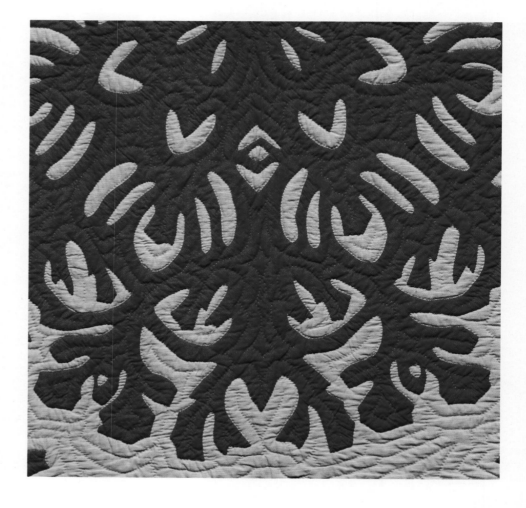

23. マモのレイ

作者不明

ハワイ諸島

19世紀末〜20世紀初頭

ホノルル美術館蔵

　〝マモ〟はサフラン科紅花の一種であり、のこぎり状の楕円型の葉の間にオレンジ色の小さい花が丸く密集して咲く。かつては観賞用またはレイを作るため、ハワイ各地で栽培されたが、現在はほとんどみられなくなった。〝マモ〟はキルトのデザインとして古典に属する方で古いキルトにこのパターンがよく使われている。マモはこのほか黒いミツスイ科の鳥の名でもあり、この鳥の黄色い羽が珍重されてこれで作ったレイをやはりマモのレイと呼ぶ。

LEI MAMO (Mamo Lei)

Maker unknown
Hawaiian Islands, late 19th century to early
　20th century
Plain woven cotton, hand applique,
straight and contour quilting
80″ (203.2cm.) × 80″ (203.2cm.)
Gift of Mr. Damon Giffard, 1959
Honolulu Academy of Arts (#2607.1)

Mamo was one of the classic patterns occasionally depicted on Hawaiian quilts in the old days. *Mamo* (*Carthamus tinctorius*) or safflower (false saffron) was an annually grown ornamental herb known for its stiff oval, dark-green, spine-toothed leaves and rounded flower heads bearing numerous small orange-yellow tubular florets. *Mamo* once was popular in Hawai'i and was cultivated mainly for its bright flowers that were made into leis. Today, cultivation has almost ceased and *mamo* flowers are rarely seen. *Mamo* originally was the name of a black Hawaiian honeycreeper (*Drepanis pacifica*) whose few bright yellow feathers above and below the tail were used in making the choicest featherworks. A *mamo* feather lei sometimes was depicted in a quilt design under the same name, Mamo Lei.

24. 葡萄のつる

作者不明
ハワイ島
19世紀末〜20世紀初頭
ホノルル美術館蔵

　英国の探検家ジョージ・ヴァンクーバー艦長は1792年いろいろな薬用植物、家畜類を満載した船でハワイを訪れた。葡萄もその時初めてハワイに紹介されたといわれている。葡萄はその後ハワイの気候風土に順応せず、栽培は現在わずかにハワイ島およびマウイ島で小規模に行われているのみである。このキルトはハワイではめずらしい葡萄の葉と実を赤でアップリケし、その上をミシンで斜めに直線でキルティングしている。同じようにミシンでキルティングした図版16の〝カイウラニの櫛〟と年代、制作場所などからみて同一作者と思われる。

KE KUMU WAINA (Grapevine)

Maker unknown
Island of Hawai'i, late 19th to early 20th
century
Plain woven cotton, hand applique, and
diagonal machine quilting
84″ (213.4cm.) × 84″ (213.4cm.)
Gift of Mrs. Richard A. Cooke, 1927
Honolulu Academy of Arts (#2589)

　The grape plant is not indigenous to Hawai'i. It was probably brought to the islands in 1792 by the English explorer Captain George Vancouver who was befriended by King Kamehameha I. However, grapevines did not grow well in the Hawaiian climate and they remained relatively rare, growing mostly in the hills outside of Hilo, Island of Hawai'i (and in recent decades on the lower slopes of Mount Haleakalā on Maui). Quilt designs based on the grapevine are not very common. In this example, a delicate quadruple-branching red grapevine with young fruit grows from the center, made of one continuous cut out piece. In contrast to this delicate appliqued pattern, rather rough machine stitching is applied in parallel lines to the entire surface. The sewing machine became available in Hawai'i in the mid-19th century. Owning a sewing machine at the time was prestigious and although hand-stitching is greatly valued today, the quilter must have felt proud to use this fancy new machine in her work.

25. パンの木

作者不明
ハワイ諸島
1930年頃
ホノルル美術館蔵

　パンの木は桑科の植物で高いものは10メートルにも達し、大きな手の平を思わせる濃緑の葉とこれまた大きな直径20センチメートル、重さ4.5キログラム近くもある実で知られている。昔からパンの木はハワイの人たちの日常生活に利用されてきた。実はつぶされて〝ポイ〟という食物になり、樹皮はタパ紙に幹の部分はくりぬかれてドラム、サーフボード、カヌーの部品などになった。このように生活上必要不可欠なパンの木はキルトのデザインとして昔から人気があり、いろいろなバリエーションでキルトを飾ってきた。パンの木のデザインでキルトを作ることは、キルター自身が成長し、豊かになり、ひいては知識を増やすことだと今でも信じられている。

パンの木
Breadfruit, 'ulu (*Artocarpus altilis*)

'ULU (Breadfruit)

Maker unknown
Hawaiian Islands, circa 1930
Plain cotton, hand applique, contour
　quilting, and machine stitched edging
84″ (213.4cm.) × 86″ (218.5cm.)
Gift of Rosalie Young Persons, 1986
Honolulu Academy of Arts (#5803.1)

　The breadfruit (*Artocarpus altilis*), a member of the mulberry family, is a strikingly tall tree (30 feet or more) with broad, luxuriant lobed leaves, that bears large round fruit weighing nearly ten pounds, measuring five to eight inches in diameter. The breadfruit tree, an excellent example of the bounty of Hawaiian nature, provides cool and comforting shade in the tropical heat and its fruit has played a traditionally important role in the daily life of the Hawaiian people. Breadfruit provided several types of basic food: the meat was mashed into a staple similar to *poi* or mixed with coconut to make pudding. From the trunk of the breadfruit tree drums (*pahu*) and surfboards (*papa he'e nalu*) were carved, as well as parts of ocean-going canoes. The bark was used to make a type of *kapa* cloth (*tapa*). The breadfruit design, reflecting this close relationship with Hawaiian life, is one of the oldest quilt patterns produced in Hawai'i and it has always been popular. Some quilters say the breadfruit pattern symbolizes "growing" and "no hunger of food, nor of wisdom." This quilt shows a simple but forceful breadfruit pattern extending into the four corners in pleasant shades of apple green. The leaves and the fruit are rendered in a relatively realistic silhouette. The piece's contour quilting is not fine but adds an interesting boldness to the design.

26. タイトル不明

作者不明
ハワイ諸島
19世紀末
ビショップ博物館蔵

　このキルトのデザインは〝やさしくお
さえて〟という名で最もよく知られてい
る。この作品は無題であるが、前出の図
版21のキルトにはその名がつけられてい
る。両者を比較するとわかるようにパタ
ーンが非常によく似ている。図版21の方
は青と白のすっきりした対照であるのに
対し、これはごく淡いピンクをオフホワ
イトに配し、コントラストはないものの
柔らかな女性的なキルトになっている。
同じデザインが〝私を忘れないで〟とい
う名で呼ばれることもある。

QUILT NAME UNKNOWN

Maker unknown
Hawaiian Islands, late 19th century
Twill woven cotton, hand applique, contour
quilting, and machine stitched edging
83″ (210cm.) × 81″ (206cm.)
Gift of Gwendolyn McBolrick, 1961
Bernice Pauahi Bishop Museum
(#1961.105.003)

This beautiful quilt is untitled, but the pattern followed by the quilter is most commonly known as *Kaomi Mālie* (Press Gently). The same design and name can be seen in quilt No. 21 in this exhibit. (In another quilt, however, a similar motif has been called "Forget-Me-Not.") In the example shown here, the pale pink of the delicate design against the white background that is slightly yellowed with age, combine to create an unusual color scheme for a Hawaian quilt.

27. タイトル不明

作者不明
ハワイ諸島
19世紀末
ビショップ博物館蔵

　テーマになっている花の名は不明である。1930年代に首府ワシントンで寄贈者の母でキルトコレクターとして知られたルイス夫人によって購入された。アップリケのパターンはミシンで縫い合わされ、ひとつの続いた葉模様のようにもみえる外側の円い輪は4つの独立した同じモチーフが上下左右でつながれたものである。植木鉢のようにみえる四隅のモチーフにかわいい小鳥が2羽ずつ止まり、中央の草花の間にもさらに小さい鳥たちがさえずっている。小鳥などの動物を扱ったハワイのキルトは非常に少なくこれは大変めずらしく、かわいい作品である。

QUILT NAME UNKNOWN

Maker unknown
Hawaiian Islands, late 19th century
Twill woven cotton, machine piecing, hand-
applique, and diagonal quilting
77″ (196cm.) × 72″ (183cm.)
Gift of Mrs. James K. Cockrell in memory of
mother Mrs. Fulton Lewis I, 1971
Bernice Pauahi Bishop Museum
(#1971.132)

　This is an unusual quilt of an unknown floral pattern. It was purchased in the Washington, D.C., area in the mid-1930s by the donor's mother, a collector of early American patchwork quilts.

　The applique pattern on this quilt is pieced together carefully by machine. The outer floral pattern is made of four separate but closely joined pieces and gives an impression of a continous semi-circle. The small bird figures among the leaves and flowers add a sweet quality to the piece.

28. タイトル不明

カウヒネ・カマラウ作
ハワイ島
1900年頃
ビショップ博物館蔵

　この作品の花のパターンは他に例をみ
ないユニークなデザインであるが、たぶ
ん作者の創造による架空の花であると思
われる。アップリケに使った布地は30イ
ンチ幅でこの時代の古い布の幅である。
キルティングの縫い目に返し針でところ
どころアクセントがつけてあり、それが
ふくらみをもち、さざ波のような効果を
上げている。

QUILT NAME UNKNOWN

Kauhine Kamalau, maker
Island of Hawai'i, circa 1900
Plain woven cotton, hand applique, contour
**　　quilting, and machine stitched edging**
81.5″ (207cm.) × 81.5″ (207cm.)
Gift of Lillian Kekauoha, 1988
Bernice Pauahi Bishop Museum
**　　(#1988.214)**

　This quilt's floral pattern is unique and, as
such, is not easily recognizable. The width of
the applique material is 30 inches, indicative
of an older fabric. Contour quilting enhanced
by small accent stitches is used to create a ripple appearance. Small knots visible at the
edge of the quilt indicate the starting point of
the quilting. This quilt is in excellent condition and does not appear to have been washed
or cleaned.

29. タイトル不明

作者不明
ハワイ島
1930年代頃
ビショップ博物館蔵

　このキルトは1930年代頃、ハワイ島の
ヒロ中学校校長であったクレイトン・チ
ャンバレン氏に贈られた。したがって一
名〝チャンバレンキルト〟として知られ
ている。パターンはパイナップルとも、
ハワイの戦士のかぶった仮面とも想像さ
れるが、このイメージがどこからきたか
は不明である。キルティングはめずらし
く返し針で縫われている。

QUILT NAME UNKNOWN

Maker unknown
Island of Hawai'i, circa 1930s
Plain woven cotton, hand applique, contour
**　quilting, and machine stitched edging**
81.5″ (207cm.) × 78″ (198cm.)
Gift of Mr. and Mrs. Clayton Chamberlain,
**　1979**
Bernice Pauahi Bishop Museum
**　(#1979.282.01)**

　This quilt was presented to Clayton J.
Chamberlain when he was principal of Hilo
Intermediate School (Island of Hawai'i) in
the 1930s. Although the name of the quilt is
unknown, it is generally referred to as the
Chamberlain Quilt.

　The quilting stitch used in this particularly
striking example is called a rocking stitch,
since the hand rocks back and forth as the
quilting is done.

30. ジャスミンの花

ハンナ・K・C・ベーカー作

オアフ島

1938年

ビショップ博物館蔵

　ジャスミンの花は白い可憐なベル状の小花で、これをつなぎ合わせたレイはハワイのレイの中でも最も特別なものとして扱われている。親しい友、知人に特別の機会に贈られて人気がある。このパターンは香り高いジャスミンの花と、これとよく似た白い小さいチューブローズを組み合わせたものである。白いレースを拡大したようにみえる作品で、1978年雑誌「グッドハウスキーピング」、アメリカ合衆国歴史協会、アメリカ工芸博物館などの主催によるキルトコンテストで最高賞を獲得した。作者のベーカー夫人はハワイのキルターとしてよく知られ、生前100に余るパターンをデザインし、30年間に彼女の教えた生徒の数は2000人にのぼるといわれる。

PĪKAKE AND TUBEROSE

Hannah Ku'umililani Cummings Baker,
**　maker**
Island of O'ahu, 1938
Plain woven cotton, hand applique, contour
quilting, and machine stitched edging
86″ (220cm.) × 86″ (220cm.)
Gift of Lillian Macedo, 1984
Bernice Pauahi Bishop Museum
**　(＃1984.423.001)**

　This quilt's design depicts two of Hawai'i's most fragrant and beloved flowers used in lei making, the *pīkake*, or jasmine, and the tuberose. In 1978 the quilt received the distinction of First Place Winner in the Great Quilts of America Competition spon-sored by *Good Housekeeping Magazine*, the United States Historical Society, and the Museum of American Folk Art.

　Mrs. Baker was a well-known quilter in Hawai'i. She learned quilting from her mother and great grandmother, and in her many years as quilter and teacher, amassed over 100 traditional and contemporary quilt patterns, which she generously shared with her students. It is estimated that over her 30 years as a quilting instructor she taught 2,000 women the art of quilting.

　Mrs. Lillian Macedo, the quilter's daugh-ter and the donor of this quilt to the Bernice Pauahi Bishop Museum, continues the tradi-tion by teaching the art of Hawaiian quilt making on the mainland.

チューブローズ　左
Tuberose *Kupaloke* (*Polianthes tuberosa*)

ジャスミンの花　右
Jasmine, *pīkake* (*Jasminum sambac*)

31. タイトル不明

作者不明
ハワイ島
1906年
ミッションハウス博物館蔵

　これはハワイ島のジェイムス・ビックネル夫妻の結婚を祝って贈られたもの。パターンはダリアの花とも、香りの高いことで知られるミウラナ（きんこうぼく）ともいわれる。中心のモチーフの位置が少しずれ、咲いている４つの花が本来のハワイアンキルトのアレンジならば四隅を向いて対角線上に並ぶのであるが、ここでは４辺の中央に向けて置かれている。このため斜線を強調するイメージでなく、むしろ円型に近いにぎやかな模様になっている。これによく似たキルトがシカゴのフィールド自然史博物館のコレクションに収められている。

QUILT NAME UNKNOWN

Maker unknown
Island of Hawai'i, 1906
Plain woven cotton, wool batting, machine piecing, hand applique and contour quilting
77″ (195.6cm.) × 79″ (200.7cm.)
Gift of Mrs. Sheila Van Zandt, 1985
Mission Houses Museum (#85.11.B8)

This is a wonderful example of the traditional Hawaiian quilt. The design is similar to the Dahlia pattern, and also closely resembles a pattern known as *Pua Miulana* (Champak Blossom). The heavily fragrant orange and white *miulana* flowers, are used in lei making as well as ingredients in perfume.

The quilter has chosen a popular pattern of the time and has changed it. The placement of this design is unusual in that the center applique has been turned 45 degrees on its axis from the diagonal to rest on the grain of the fabric. As a result, the middle pairs of flowers in the border design had to be altered to fit the new arrangement, changing the symmetry of the design. A similar quilt is now in the collection of the Field Museum of Natural History, Chicago, Illinois. The identity of the quilt maker is unknown, but other quilts from the same family were made in Hāwī, North Kohala, Island of Hawai'i. According to the donor, this quilt was a wedding gift to Mr. and Mrs. James Bicknell in 1906.

32. タイトル不明

作者不明
ハワイ島
1910年頃
ミッションハウス博物館蔵

このキルトは前ページに紹介されたジェームス・ビックネルのキルトに4年遅れて、その弟のディヴス・ビックネルにやはり結婚式の贈り物として作られた。兄弟が育ったハワイ島コハラにあるコハラさとうきび農場に当時働いていた女性たちの作といわれている。百合の花がモチーフと思われるが、デザインは比較的シンプルで赤と白の古典的な配色が美しい作品である。

QUILT NAME UNKNOWN

Maker unknown
Island of Hawai'i, circa 1910
Plain woven cotton, wool batting, machine
   piecing, hand applique, and contour
   quilting
79.5″ (201.9cm.) × 79.5″ (201.9cm.)
Gift of Mrs. Frank E. Wilson
   (Ellen Bicknell), 1979
Mission Houses Museum (#79.2.B8)

This unique quilt design bears some similarity to the various lily patterns. Here, the border and the central medallion form an integral design. The relatively simple pattern, with exposed ground fabric combined with the red on white color scheme, is typical of early quilt designs. The strong diagonals emphasize the method of cutting the applique by first folding the fabric into eighths.

According to his daughter, this quilt was given to Joseph Davis Bicknell as a wedding gift in 1910 "... by some woman who had worked on the plantation he was raised on." The brother of James Bicknell, Joseph Davis Bicknell, grew up on the Kohala Sugar Plantation at Hāwī, North Kohala, on the Island of Hawai'i. Kohala Plantation was begun by the Bicknells' missionary grandfather, the Reverend Elias Bond, to provide supplementary income for the mission station.

33. タイトル不明

作者不明
ハワイ諸島
19世紀末～20世紀初頭
ドーターズオブハワイ資料館蔵

使われているモチーフはばらと思われる。ばらは1882年以前にハワイへ持ち込まれた外来の植物であるが、女王エマの夏の宮殿はそのばらの庭園で有名である。色の変わるばらとして知られる特別種は女王の名をとって〝クィーンエマロケラニ〟と名づけられている。外側の花びらは黒に近い赤で内側へいくにしたがって赤からピンクに変わるのでめずらしがられる。クィーンエマはカメハメハ大王の系統をひく最後の女王で、このあとを継いだカラカウオ王は、ハワイ政治上初めて選挙で選ばれた王であった。この政権交替に際し、クィーンエマを支持する一派がカラカウオ王に投票した議員たちを議場で襲うなどという血に染まった一幕もあった。このクィーンエマの夏の宮殿が現在この作品を所有するドーターズオブハワイの本部である。

ロケラニのバラ
Rose, *lokelani* (*Rosaceae rosa*)

QUILT NAME UNKNOWN

Maker unknown
Hawaiian Islands, late 19th century to early
   20th century
Plain woven cotton, wool batting, hand and
   machine piecing, hand applique, and
   contour quilting
77.5″ (195.8cm.) × 77.5″ (195.8cm.)
Gift of Mr. and Mrs. Thomas Guard, Jr.,
   1962
Daughters of Hawai'i (#680),
   Queen Emma Summer Palace

The flowers depicted in this quilt are probably roses which were introduced to the Hawaiian Islands prior to 1822. Queen Emma's Summer Palace, Hānaiakamalama in Hawaiian, was noted for its lovely rose garden, and there was a certain rose named after Queen Emma, the *lokelani*. This variety of rose was referred to as *loke wai kāhuli* (rose with changing color) as its petals were dark on the outside and light in the center. The palace garden was planned by a distinguished Danish landscape architect, H. Augustus de Holstein, in the late 1850s or early 1860s. In 1913, when the Daughters of Hawai'i took over the care of Hānaiakamalama, it was noted that there were great quantities of roses on the terrace.

34. ログキャビン

ジョセフ・マキニの祖母の作
カウアイ島
1850年頃
ホノルル美術館蔵

　アメリカ本土のログキャビンのパターンを作者なりに変型して作った大変めずらしい作品である。ログキャビン特有の〝光と影〟すなわち明暗の色を黄、赤、青で使い分け、ブロックも非常に大きく、大胆な構図になっている。本土のログキャビンによく見られる精密に計算しつくされたパターンの動きはなく、むしろ即興的に手の動くまま、心のうつるままにデザインしたような感がある。グレイの縞の部分は紺の布が変色したものでこれが思いがけないバリエーションとなり、楽しいリズムをそえている。

LOG CABIN

Great-grandmother of Joseph Makini, maker
Island of Kaua'i, circa 1850
Plain woven cotton, hand piecing, and hand
**　quilting**
80″ (203cm.) × 79″ (199.5cm.)
Gift of Mrs. Joseph Makini, 1946
Honolulu Academy of Arts (#5023.1)

　The great majority of Hawaiian quilt designs are unique and owe little or nothing to mainland models. This quilt is unusual in that it is based on the Log Cabin patchwork quilts extremely popular on the mainland in the 19th century. A fascinating optical effect of light and shadow is created by the systematic arrangement of square blocks made of light and dark colored strips, or "logs," combined in a manner that suggests a log cabin structure.

　In this example, the usual pattern has been adapted by a Hawaiian quilter who has enlarged her blocks to almost twice the size of traditional designs. The quilter's colors are as bold as her patterns are huge, bright Hawaiian yellow and orange for light portions, and blue and red for the dark areas. Sections of the blue fabric used in the quilt have faded under the strong Hawaiian sun to produce a pleasant grey. The arrangement of light and shadow is less strictly regulated than is usual in the traditional Log Cabin pattern. These unexpected elements combine to produce a lively Hawaiian image with a visual rhythm all its own.

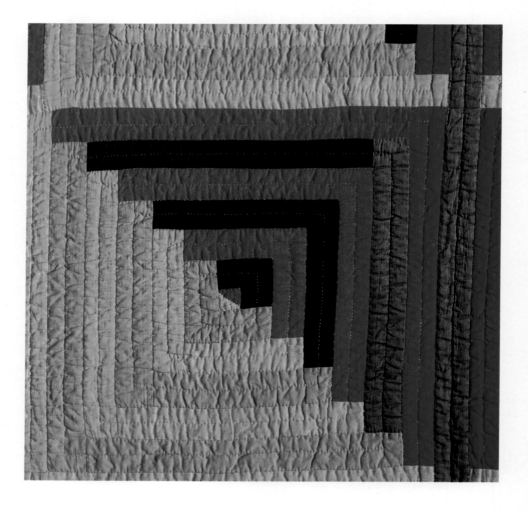

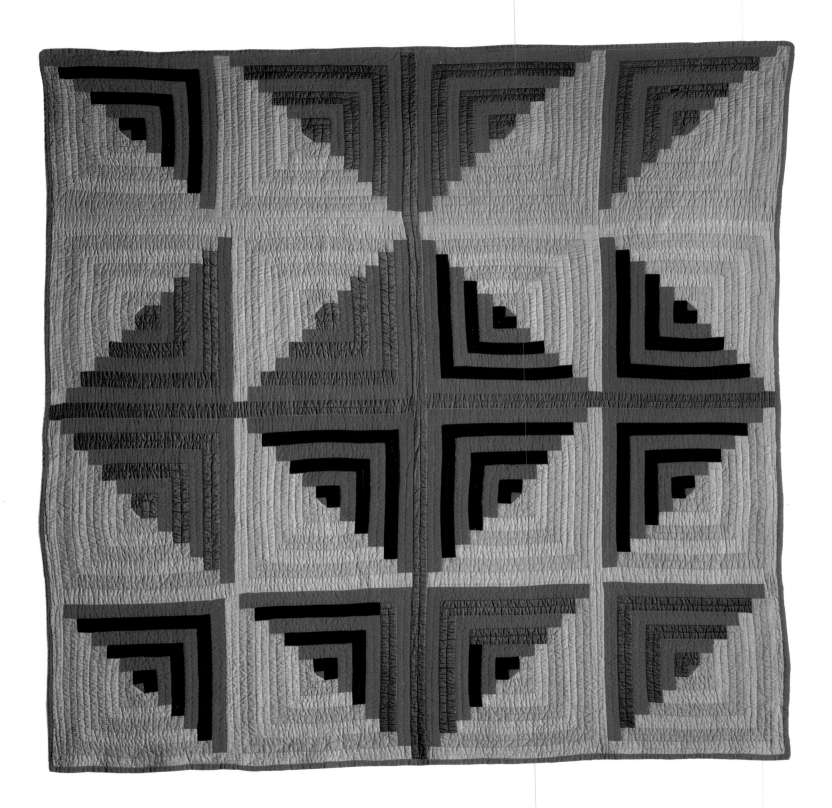

35. まがったひざ

作者不明
カウアイ島
19世紀末～20世紀初頭
ホノルル美術館蔵

　円型が多いハワイのキルトパターンの中で、一味違うジグザグ模様である。はっきりとした赤、青、白を使い、横に流れる線を強調する力強い作品である。このジグザグパターンはワワケの樹皮から作られたカパ（他の太平洋地域ではタパと呼ぶ）にプリントされた木版模様によくみられる。初期のハワイのキルトはカパの模様を手がかりにデザインしたものが多く、特にキルティングの線はカパのパターンをそのまままねたものがたくさんある。ハワイ語でキルトの事をカパアパナ（アップリケをしたカパ）と呼ぶことからも察することができる。

KULI PU'U (Bent Knee)

Maker unknown
Island of Kaua'i, late 19th century to early
**　20th century**
Plain woven cotton, hand piecing, hand
applique, hand quilting, and machine-
stitch edging
92″ (233.7cm.) × 82″ (208.2cm.)
Gift of Mrs. Charles M. Cooke, 1929
Honolulu Academy of Arts (#2813)

　The unusually bold design of this quilt, including dynamic zig-zag patterns of contrasting red, blue, and white, creates a remarkable image of released energy, a rarity within the Hawaiian tradition of well-balanced, inward-looking quilts. The zig-zag pattern has been popular in Hawai'i, frequently used in *tapa (kapa)* making. *Kapa*, a non-woven paper-like fabric made of the inner bark of the *wauke* or *māmaki* plant, was produced on the Hawaiian Islands long before the period of Western contact. As clothing and bed coverings, *kapa* provided Hawaiians with warmth and protection as well as visual delight. It is probable that when missionary wives introduced American quilting to Hawai'i, the long familiar patterns of *kapa* inspired Hawaiian quilters. Interestingly, in the old days, Hawaiians called the cotton cloth quilt *kapa āpana*, ''*kapa* with applied design.'' *Kuli Pu'u* is printed on the reverse side of the quilt on one corner, confirming the design name.

36. ガーデンアイランド　モキハナ

作者不明
カウアイ島
20世紀初頭
ホノルル美術館蔵

　1904年、カウアイ島の週間新聞〝ガーデンアイランド〟の処女発行を記念して、カウアイ島だけに生育するモキハナを模様にひとつのキルトが誕生した。作者はマヒコア夫人といわれるが異説もある。最初のガーデンアイランドのキルトは白地に赤のモキハナ模様であったと伝えられるが、のちにパターンはたびたび借用された。この作品は白地に緑でむしろ実物の色に近い。モキハナは島の雨の多い山地にのみ生育する灌木で、その小さい青い実をつないでレイにする。特殊な匂いがあり、肌にふれると炎症を起こすこともある。一見めだたない植物であるがカウアイ島にのみ育つことから〝島花〟になっている。

モキハナの実で作ったレイ
Mokihana (Pelea anisata)

GARDEN ISLAND, MOKIHANA

Maker unknown
Island of Kaua'i, early 20th century
**Plain woven cotton, hand applique, and
　　contour quilting**
83.5″ (212.1cm.) × 81.5″ (205cm.)
Gift of Mrs. Dora Isenberg, 1940
Honolulu Academy of Arts (#4832)

　When *"The Garden Island,"* the first weekly newspaper on the island of Kaua'i began publication in 1904, a quilt called the Garden Island or *Kīhāpai Pua* (flower garden) was created to commemorate this event. The creation of this design has been attributed to several quilters. It is believed the original design was red and white with a floral pattern suggesting fruit of the *mokihana* tree. In following years, the pattern became popular and was adopted by other quilters who sometimes substituted blue, or in this case green, for the original red. This particular quilt has the additional title *Mokihana*, specifically indicating the design source. *Mokihana* is a small tree *(Pelea anisata)* of the rain forest peculiar to the Island of Kaua'i. The tree's small leathery fruits, which have an anise-like fragrance, were strung into leis and garlands. *Mokihana*, in the "Song of the Lei of the Hawaiian Islands," is the emblem of Kaua'i and it seems appropriate to use this motif to remember an important event in the modern history of Kaua'i.

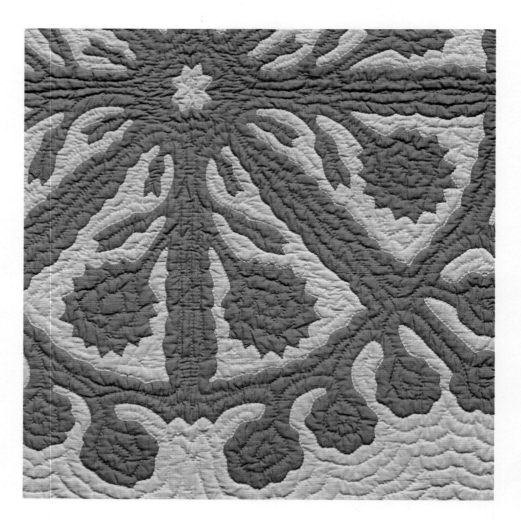

37. ナウィリウィリの美

ジョージ・モンゴメリー夫人作
カウアイ島
1930年頃
ホノルル美術館蔵

　正方形でなく矩形のキルトはこの年代のものとしてはめずらしい。白地にくすんだグレイグリーンで〝錨〟が中央に4つ、まわりに6つ、一見すると花模様かと見まがうほど、繊細に表現されている。錨がテーマになっているのは、このキルトがカウアイ島東南の海岸ナウィリナウィリ湾に初めて港ができたのを祝って作られたからである。錨というどちらかといえば男性的なモチーフ。それを使いながらデリケートな線描に近いモチーフの扱い方、柔らかい中間色の利用などで優しい、女性らしい作品になっている。

NĀWILIWILI BEAUTY

Mrs. George Montgomery, maker
Island of Kaua'i, circa 1930
Plain woven cotton, hand applique, and
**　contour quilting**
91″ (231.1cm.) × 61″ (154.9cm.)
Gift of Mrs. Dora Isenberg, 1940
Honolulu Academy of Arts (#4831)

　Some Hawaiian quilts were made in commemoration of a particular event. On this unusually shaped rectangular quilt, pale grey-green anchor patterns are set against a white background. As the anchors suggest, the quilt commemorates a nautical scene, in this case the opening of a new harbor at Nāwiliwili Bay on the southeast coast of the Island of Kaua'i. The quilt was made by Mrs. George Montgomery, a noted quilter of Līhu'e, Kaua'i.

　Mrs. Montgomery cleverly combines anchor shapes and curved foliage patterns into an overall encircling flower-like image, a design arrangement familiar to Hawaiian quilts. In spite of the quilt's masculine subject matter, the pastel colors on white and the intricacy of the design are unmistakably feminine. The contour quilting throughout the piece is extremely fine, demonstrating the extraordinary skill of this admired quilter.

モキハナクラブでキルトを教えるジョージモンゴメリー夫人、1933年
Mrs. George Montgomery, seated at the far right, demonstrates her quilting at the Mokihana Club, March 1, 1933. (Photograph courtesy of the Kaua'i Museum)

Contemporary Quilts

38. フキラウ　または魚とさんご礁

デザイン：エリザベス・アカナ

作：メイベル・オリヴィエラ

オアフ島

1973年

フキラウは網に〝テイ〟の葉を結び、浅瀬でこれを引き、さんご礁の中の色とりどりの魚を捕獲するハワイの伝統的な魚とりの手法である。このキルトは青い海を象徴する水色の地をバックにさんご礁や海草の間の魚たちを無心に泳がせ、それを中央で丸くかこんで網を表した楽しい作品である。四隅のはさみをもたげた蟹がさりげないユーモアをそえている。

HUKILAU OR FISH ON CORAL

Elizabeth Akana, designer; Mabel Oliveira, maker
Island of O'ahu, 1973
Plain woven cotton/polyester, hand applique, and contour quilting
112″ (284cm.) × 118″ (300cm.)
Elizabeth Akana, owner

Hukilau is the Hawaiian expression for pulling *(huki)* a net with attached leaves *(lau)*, to drive fish into shallow water. In earlier times, when the fish supply in the coral reefs was more plentiful, *hukilau* was an important traditional method of fishing. Many species of fish would be caught including *'ama'ama* (mullet), *moili'i* (threadfish), *'ōpelu* (mackerel scad), and *mālolo* (flying fish), all of which formed a significant part of the Hawaiian diet.

This quilt reflects the relationship of Hawaiians to the sea. Fish, coral, and underwater plants are depicted within the aqua-colored ocean. The circular orientation of the motifs suggests the traditional method of the *hukilau*, in which fish are surrounded and subsequently trapped in the net.

39. イリマのレイ

作：シャーロット・L・カスカート
デザイン：デボラ・カカリア
オアフ島
1984年

　近づく初孫の誕生を心待ちにしていたある日、シャーロットの胸にイリマを唄ったハワイの歌のメロディーが何度も流れた。やがて生まれてきた彼女の初孫はそれにちなんでイリマと名づけられ、彼女はイリマをテーマにキルトを作った。このキルトはイリマが成長し、人生の重要な節目を迎える時に祖母から贈られることになっている。

　黄色い、小さいイリマの花はオアフ島の島花であり、かつては王族のレイとして使われた。一本のレイを作るのに約2000個の花がいるといわれ、現在では特別な機会にのみ人びとの胸元を飾る。このキルトはイリマの花と葉をセンターと周囲に配し、その間にシダと組み合わせたイリマのレイを2本、やや写実的に華やかに表現している。

イリマの花のレイ
'Ilima Lei (*Sida fallax*)

LEI 'ILIMA ('Ilima Lei)

Charlotte Leimakani Cathcart, maker;
**　Deborah Kakalia, designer**
Island of O'ahu, 1984
Plain woven cotton/polyester, hand
**　applique, and contour quilting**
99″ (251cm.) × 102″ (259cm.)
Charlotte L. Cathcart, owner

　While thinking about the imminent arrival of a new grandchild, the quilter recalled a Hawaiian song that begins with the words "O ka 'ilima." The baby was given the name *Lei 'ilima*, and this quilt, her namesake, will be presented to her one day to commemorate an important event in her life.

　The *'ilima* flower ranges in color from yellow to orange to red and, in its yellow form, is the official flower of the Island of O'ahu. The blossom is delicate and thin and often 800 are used to make a lei. The quilt pattern is based on repeated rectangular shapes and incorporates both the individual *'ilima* flowers in gold and yellow as well as entwined leis.

40. ココナッツとパイナップル

メアリイ・カラマ作
オアフ島
1973年

　ココナッツは古くからハワイの人びとの日常生活に欠かせない資源として数多くの物に利用されてきた。パイナップルもハワイの産物として特に有名である。このキルトをそうしたおなじみのハワイのテーマを素直に写実的に表現している。キルトの中心を大地とみなし、そこからパイナップルが生え、その間にココナッツの木が弧を描いて大きな葉を空に向けて左右に広げる。中心は多少複雑に、周囲に近くなるほどシンプルになるデザイン構成も非常に効果をあげている。

ココナッツ
Coconut palm, *niu* (*Cocos nucifera*)

COCONUT AND PINEAPPLE

Meali'i Kalama, maker and designer
Island of O'ahu, 1973
Plain woven cotton/polyester, hand
**　　applique, and contour quilting**
108″ (274cm.) × 108″ (274cm.)
Meali'i Kalama, owner

　The coconut palm *(niu)*, probably brought by the first Polynesian settlers to Hawai'i, was a significant source of raw materials essential to the lives of early Hawaiians. Posts for houses as well as large hula drums were made from the trunks while roof thatching and fans were fabricated from the leaves. Sennit, a strong lashing material, was produced from the husk, and *haupia*, a still popular dessert, came from the meat of the coconut. The pineapple *(halakahiki)*, now a major commercial crop for which Hawai'i has become famous, was first introduced to the islands in 1813.

　This contemporary quilt design is based on stylized representations of the pineapple and coconut palm. Pineapples are placed around the center, seemingly close to the earth, while the palm trees sway above protectively, symbolic of the ways in which these plants have nurtured the people of Hawai'i.

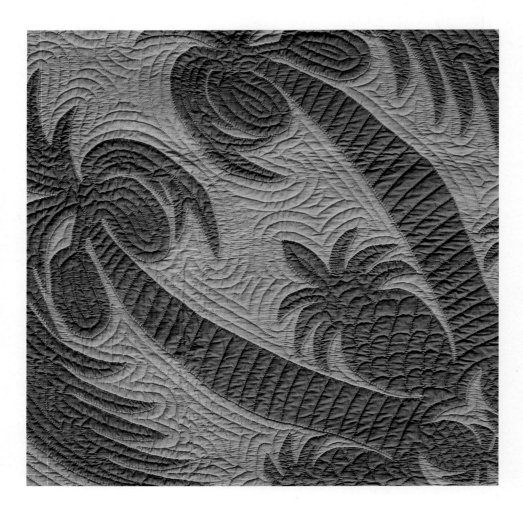

41. 謙譲の美

メアリイ・カラマ作

オアフ島

1985年

　ホノルル市クィーン医療センターの庭にあるボンバックスの木は毎年1月から5月まで大きくあざやかなピンクの花を咲かせる。この花をテーマにして、病める人をいたわり、保護するというセンターの機能を丸くおさめたデザイン構成で象徴している。花の色のピンクはここでは白に変わり、病院にふさわしい清潔な感じを出している。ボンバックスの花のデザインの間に丸い未開のシダの葉がアレンジされているのは作者が好んで使うサインがわりの印章であり、彼女が人生のモットーとする謙譲の意を表している。

ボンバックスの花
Bombax (*Bombax ellipticum*)

KA U'I O MEALI'I
(The Beauty of Meali'i)

Meali'i Kalama, maker and designer
Island of O'ahu, 1985
Plain woven cotton/polyester, hand
　applique, and contour quilting
102″ (259cm.) × 102″ (259cm.)
Meali'i Kalama, owner

　On the grounds of the Queen's Medical Center in Honolulu, a bombax tree *(Bombax ellipticum)* grows. Blossoms emerge from January to May and it is said that the buds open with a bursting sound. A depiction of this flower is one motif in the design of this quilt.

The bombax tree is near a hospital, so the quilter chose rounded shapes to enclose the flower and to express the idea of care-giving, one function of a hospital. The design is symbolic and not only represents plant life, but also an abstract idea. *Kaona* (hidden meaning) is present in other Hawaiian arts, and it has been consciously introduced into this quilt. Moreover, Meali'i has incorporated the tight curve of an un-opened fern leaf, symbolizing the humility for which she strives, as her logo or permanent visual signature. The contemporary Hawaiian quilt therefore can be appreciated on different levels: as representing elements from nature, as a pattern of lines and shapes, and as a symbol, if the hidden meaning is known.

42. チャイニーズマネーツリー

キャロル・D・カマイレ作

オアフ島

1976〜1981年

　この現代感覚にあふれたキルトはキャロル独自のデザインで、しかも処女作といってもいい初期の作品である。ハワイ各地にみられる、俗にチャイニーズマネーツリーと呼ばれる観葉植物のとがった葉先をイメージに、それを中心から四方へ広げて全体を大きな花びらのような形で大胆にまとめている。『作品を手放す時は一夜その下で眠ってから、そうすれば私の "愛" がキルトと共に新しい持ち主に届けられるから』と彼女は言う。

中国銭の木
Chinese Money Tree, *hala - pepe*
(*Dracaena acuminata*)

CHINESE MONEY TREE

Carol Dowling Kamaile, maker and designer
Island of O'ahu, 1976-1981
Plain woven cotton/polyester, hand applique
**　contour quilting**
100″ (254cm.) × 100″ (254cm.)
Carol D. Kamaile, owner

　This is the first quilt made by Carol Kamaile, and the Chinese Money Tree *(Dracaena acuminata)* is her own original design. In this bold pattern, eight rigid stalks with spiky bracts push into four heart-shaped corners. The composition extends to the quilt's edges where it is encased by a narrow border.

　Carol came to the islands in 1963 and quickly was taken by the beauty of Hawaiian quilting. In 1976, a friend, Luika Kamaka, inspired her to begin quilting and to develop her own design framework. According to Carol who now teaches, ''I love being able to create new patterns for my students and myself. Before I release a quilt for sale, I sleep under it at least one time so that my love will go with the quilt.''

43. パンの木

キャシー・中島作
静岡県御殿場市
1989年

　パンの木はハワイアンキルトの最もポピュラーなパターンのひとつである。食用としても用いられ、木工品の素材としても多く使われるパンの木は、なんといっても強い太陽光線をさえぎり、人びとに涼しく心地よい木陰を提供してくれるありがたい木でもある。数年前、彼女がオアフ島の田舎のレストランで食事をしたとき、壁にパンの木のハワイアンキルトがかけてあり、その素晴らしさに強く心を打たれ、「いつの日にか、私もパンの木に挑戦する」と心に決めて、取り組んだのがこの作品である。日本のむら染めの生地を素材にしている。

BREADFRUIT

Kathy Nakajima, maker and designer
Gotemba, Japan, 1989
Plain woven cotton, hand dyed, hand
applique, and contour quilting
106″ (270cm.) × 106″ (270cm.)
Kathy Nakajima, owner

　The breadfruit tree serves many functions in Hawai'i. It is used for shade, food, and wooden objects and is a significant design source for Hawaiian quilts. In reference to the beginnings of Hawaiian quilting, one often hears the story of a woman who upon seeing the shadow of breadfruit leaves cast upon a sheet, traced the outlines, cut it out, and appliqued the pattern to a plain backing. It is believed that from this prototype, the bold, vegetative Hawaiian quilt designs flourished. It is also told that if the first quilt one makes is of the breadfruit pattern, one's talents will be abundant.

　Because of a long and notable history, there are a variety of quilt patterns based on the breadfruit tree. While visiting Hawai'i, her homeland, Kathy was stirred by a quilt of the breadfruit pattern and upon returning to Japan, created her interpretation of the tree. Concentrating on the elements of leaves and fruit for her design, Kathy uses hand dyed blue cotton which, with its changeable tones, gives a light and shadow effect to the quilt.

44. 母の日

キャシー・中島作
静岡県御殿場市
1989年

　作品のモチーフはカーネーション。日本では「母の日」（5月の第2日曜日）にカーネーションを贈り、母の健康と長寿を祈るが、ハワイではよくレイにして、親愛のシンボルとしてまわりの人びとにプレゼントをする。カーネーションがハワイで栽培されるようになったのはごく近年で、そもそもは外来の花のようである。あれだけ多くの花が乱れ咲き、その美しさを競い合っているハワイの花の中でも、彼女は特にカーネーションが大好きである。この花を見ると、遠いハワイの思い出がよみがえってくる気がするからであると彼女はいう。

MOTHER'S DAY

Kathy Nakajima, maker and designer
Gotemba, Japan, 1989
Plain woven cotton, hand dyed, hand
**　　applique, and contour quilting**
53″ (135cm.) × 71″ (180cm.)
Kathy Nakajima, owner

　The floral theme of this quilt is the carnation. A flower well known for its spicy fragrance, the carnation is often used in Hawai'i to make leis. Even though it was recently introduced to the islands, it has a Hawaiian name, *poni mōʻi*. This is based on two words, *poni*, meaning to crown, and *mōʻi*, a king, which combine to make the word coronation. Initially, the sound in English of the word carnation was confused with coronation, and thus, the Hawaiian name for the flower developed.

　To commemorate the special feeling of Mother's Day, Kathy has created a charming representation of carnations. The intricate arrangement of petals, stems, and leaves forms a fascinating design and shows full blossoms resting atop sturdy stems. This central design is encompassed by an unusual wavy border. A traditional Hawaiian color scheme of red-on-white is selected, but the softly-colored, hand-dyed red fabric creates a delicate and subtle expression.

45.谷間の百合

ウィルマ・C・ジェンセンとキャサリーン・
P・ニシダ作

ハワイ島

1960〜1984年

　この作品は母娘二代にわたる力作であ
る。アップリケの過程までは母親のウィ
ルマ・ジェンセンが1960年頃に完成し、
そのまま手つかずに20数年が経過。やっ
と1984年娘のキャサリーンがキルティン
グの部分を終わらせてこのキルトが誕生
した。"谷間の百合"のパターンはたびた
びハワイアンキルトに使われ、バリエー
ションもいろいろである。ここではシダ
と組み合わされ、特徴ある鈴の形をした
"谷間の百合"が中心から繊細な姿を四
方にのばす。色はハワイアンキルトの伝
統通り、華やかな紅と白である。

LILY OF THE VALLEY

Kathleen Puanani Nishida and
**　Wilma C. Jensen, makers**
Island of Hawai'i, 1960-1984
Plain woven cotton, hand applique, and
**　contour quilting**
100″ (254cm.) × 104″ (264cm.)
Kathleen Puanani Nishida, owner

　This quilt has very special meaning for
Kathleen Nishida as it represents the combined efforts of her mother, Wilma C. Jensen, and herself. Wilma began making this
quilt in the early 1960s, and it remained in the
applique stage until 1984 when Kathleen fi-
nally completed the last stitches.

　The Lily of the Valley motif is traditional
and it has been featured on Hawaiian quilts
for many years, hence there are several variations. In this example, four main flower
stems, identifiable by the hanging bell-shaped
blossoms, extend along the diagonal axis. In
keeping with traditional Hawaiian quilt designs, a bold red-on-white color scheme has
been used.

46. うたういるか

キャサリーン・P・ニシダとロビン・K・ジェンセン作

ハワイ島

1988年

マウナケアビーチホテル蔵

　このいかにも楽しいキルトは、ハワイ島マウナケアビーチホテルの所蔵品でキャサリーン、ロビン姉弟の共作である。デザイン化されたいるかが2頭ずつ4組になり、波頭の間でくちばしをそろえて合唱するかのようにみえる。カーブするいろいろな線を上手に組み合わせ、それがダイナミックな円型としてよくまとまっている。非常に現代的な題材であるが、コントアキルティングのテクニックと海にちなんだテーマにふさわしい白と青の二色だけで仕上げた点は、やはりハワイアンキルトの伝統に因んだ作品といえるであろう。

SINGING DOLPHINS

Kathleen Puanani Nishida and
**　Robin Keli'i Jensen, makers and designers**
Island of Hawai'i, 1988
Plain woven cotton, hand applique, and
**　contour quilting**
92″ (234cm.) × 92″ (234cm.)
Mauna Kea Beach Hotel, owner

　Kathleen and her brother Robin are challenged by the designing and making of contemporary Hawaiian quilts. They work together to generate concepts and to resolve the dynamics of an interactive design. A representative from the Mauna Kea Beach Hotel came to the Waimea Hawaiian Quilt Club and asked for submissions. Kathy and Robin designed and made Singing Dolphins, now part of the hotel's collection of 30 quilts.

　The use of curvilinear shapes within the design creates a flow which carries the viewer's eye throughout the quilt's composition. The repetition of the stylized dolphin tails and wave tips are important design elements and unify the pattern as a whole. A contemporary theme is expressed, yet important Hawaiian quilt traditions are maintained by the techniques of design as well as by the use of two solid, contrasting colors.

47. ハイレワの美しい蓮

ドリス・I・F・ノサカ作

ハワイ島

1984～1986年

　蓮の花の強い生命力、すなわち暗い沼底から生長し、ほとんど同時にたくさんの茎が蕾をつけ、それが花開き実をつけるたくましさ、すばらしさを、ドリスは子供の頃母の家の蓮池で見た時から特別な印象を持った。この思い出がハイレワの小さな沼で蓮の花を再び見つけた時によみがえり、キルトが誕生した。柔らかい中間色でまとめたこの作品はちょうど蓮池を上からのぞくような詩的な印象をあたえる。

KA HASU NANI O HALE'IWA
(The Beautiful Lotus of Hale'iwa)

**Doris Iwalani Feary Nosaka, maker and
　　designer**
Island of Hawai'i, 1984-1986
**Plain woven cotton, hand applique, and
　　contour quilting**
101″ (257cm.) × 103″ (262cm.)
Doris Nosaka, owner

　In her childhood, Doris Nosaka lived in Moanalua, Island of O'ahu, on land given to her grandmother by Princess Ruth Ke'e-likolani. Within the vast grounds of Princess Ruth's home, Keawemālie, were natural artesian springs and ponds where water lilies and lotuses grew in abundance. The quilter marvelled then, as she does now, "...at the ability of the wonderous lotus to bud, blossom, and seed simultaneously while growing out of deep mud on the bottom of ponds." The memory of the plant stayed with her, and in later years Doris came upon a small pond in Hale'iwa where lotuses also grew. Seeing the lotus again provided inspiration for this quilt.

　The soft aqua color against an olive green background creates the impression of looking into a lotus pond. The lyrical mingling of leaves, buds, and flowers forms a unique depiction of *ka hasu nani*.

115

48. ハワイの有名なレフア

作：アネッテ・スマダ

デザイン：エレノア・アフナ

ハワイ島

1984年

　ハワイ各地にみられる赤いレフアの花はキラウエア火山の女神ペレの好んだ花として知られている。『山に登る時にはレフアの花を摘んではいけない。手折るなら帰り道になさい。そうしないとペレの怒りで山は雨と霧に包まれて迷子になります。』とハワイの人たちは言う。このキルトは1984年フラのコンテストとして知られるメリーモナーク祭に記念して作られたもので、歌や、フラダンスに多く引用されるレフアの花と葉の細部がアップリケとキルティングでていねいに表現されている。

KAULANA KA LEHUA O HAWAI'I
(The Famous Lehua of Hawai'i)

Annette Sumada, maker; Eleanor Ahuna, designer
Island of Hawai'i, 1984
Plain woven cotton, hand applique, and contour quilting
88″ (224cm.) × 88″ (224cm.)
Annette Sumada, owner

The showy red '*ōhi*'*a lehua* is the flower of the Island of Hawai'i. Hawaiians also consider this flower sacred to Pele, the legendary volcano goddess who resides on Mount Kīlauea. Islanders say when one goes to the mountains to gather flowers, *lehua* should be picked only on the return journey, otherwise an offended Pele will envelop that person in rain and mist.

This quilt pattern was designed by Eleanor Ahuna to commemorate the 1984 Merrie Monarch Festival, an annual hula competition in Hilo honoring the late King David Kalākaua. The quilt demonstrates a contemporary quilting technique in that stitches are used to define the overlapping of leaves and branches. Close scrutiny reveals the presence of buds, flowers, and seed capsules, parts of the tree that is greatly celebrated in song and dance. The quilter says, "My preference on designs leans toward the old and traditional patterns. I believe that these beautiful quilts should be treasured, but also used and enjoyed today, and not folded and put away in the closet."

レフアの花
Lehua, haole (Calliandra inaequilatera)

49. ハレアカラの銀のつるぎ

アネッテ・スマダ作
ハワイ島
1986年

　図版50と同じ〝銀のつるぎ〟をテーマにしている。この特殊な植物は銀色の葉で知られ、かつてはハレアカラ山上に群生して、月夜には雪山を思わせる銀世界を出現させていたが、今は絶滅の危機にさらされている。〝銀のつるぎ〟はハワイ語で〝アヒナヒナ〟と呼ばれ、灰色を意味する、キルトのテーマとしてもたびたび登場する。この作品は〝銀のつるぎ〟が長い長い何年もの未熟の状態を経過し、やっと一生を終える前の一瞬、花開いたところを表現したものである。

開花した銀のつるぎ
Silversword (*Argyroxiphium sandwicense*)

'ĀHINAHINA O HALEAKALĀ
(The Silversword of Haleakalā)

Annette Sumada, maker
Island of Hawai'i, 1986
Plain woven cotton, hand applique, and
**　contour quilting**
110″ (279cm.) × 110″ (270cm.)
Jiro Alan Sumada, owner

The bold lines and cool colors of this quilt represent Maui's distinctive plant, the silversword. Once growing in such abundance on the slopes of Mount Haleakalā as to make the landscape look like winter bathed in moonlight, this endemic plant is now on the verge of extinction and has aroused the concern of naturalists. The silvery, hairy leaves give rise to the plant's name, 'āhinahina, meaning grey in Hawaiian.

This is a traditional pattern recreated by many quilters over the years. Here four main plants form a cross in the center with smaller silversword plants placed around the border. This is a special depiction of 'āhinahina because the plant grows as a small bush for a number of years, then, with a burst, it flowers and dies. The quilt's center captures that one distinct season for 'āhinahina, when the plant shows its splendor and is in full bloom.

50. 銀のつるぎ

ジュネデイレ・L・クイノリス作
ハワイ島
1961年

　"アヒナヒナ"または"銀のつるぎ"と呼ばれるハワイの特殊な植物はハワイ島の高山植物で特にハレアカラ山の火口付近に多く育つので知られている。乾燥した空気と寒暖の差の激しいハレアカラの気候の中で、何年かは灰色の丸みをおびた形でとどまり（10年から14年の間といわれる）そして突然ある年、長い茎をのばし、花をつけ、その花が枯れると一生が終わる。このキルトはまだ花をつけていないうずくまるような形の"アヒナヒナ"を周囲からのばし、それを"ウル"で結んでこの植物の強い長い生命力を表現している。木の葉のようなキルティングの模様は"亀の背"といわれるカウアイ独特のキルティング手法である。

銀のつるぎ
Silversword (*Argyroxiphium sandwicense*)

'ĀHINAHINA (Silversword)

Junedale Lauwaeomakana Quinories, maker
Island of Hawai'i, 1961
Plain woven cotton/polyester, hand
applique, and *kuahonu* (turtle's back)
quilting
97″ (246cm.) × 97″ (246cm.)
Junedale L. Quinories, owner

　In the Hawaiian language '*āhinahina* means grey. It is also the name given to the silversword, an endemic Hawaiian plant which grows in dry areas on volcanic cinders in Haleakalā Crater on the Island of Maui. It is well-adapted to high elevations, hot temperatures during summer days, temperatures below freezing on winter nights, and a low level of rainfall throughout the year. The remarkable silversword remains in a rounded form for 9 to 14 years when it produces one tall flower stalk and then dies.

　This traditional quilt pattern represents the rounded form of the '*āhinahina*. The eight individual motifs, placed near the outer edges, are connected to one another by a thick vine, well illustrating the strength and tenacity of the '*āhinahina*, which thrives despite a difficult environment.

121

51. たばこの葉と花

ジュネデイレ・L・クイノリス作
ハワイ島
1983年

　タバコがアメリカからハワイにもたら
されたのは1812年頃で、ハワイ島のコナ
地域で栽培されたが、商業的には成功し
なかった。このパターンはその頃初めて
作られたものかもしれない。４つの花び
んの中にタバコの葉と花が生けられてい
るが、その茎の分かれ方、花のありさま、
アーチ形につながった葉など写実とは離
れてデザインの面白さを追った作品であ
る。

KA PIKA WAI O KA LAU PAKA
(The Vase of Tobacco Leaves and Flowers)

Junedale Lauwaeomakana Quinories, maker
Island of Hawai'i, 1983
Plain woven cotton, hand applique, and
**　contour quilting**
93.5″ (237cm.) × 111.5″ (283cm.)
Adam Quinories, owner

　Curiously, this may be a traditional pattern. Tobacco (*paka*) from America was introduced to Hawai'i in 1812 and was grown,
unsuccessfully, as a commercial crop in the
Kona area of the Island of Hawai'i from approximately 1908 to 1929. This design
presumably dates from that period.

　Primarily, four vases holding tobacco
plants are represented. The freedom of interpretation in Hawaiian quilting designs is
visible in the divided main flower stem, in the
placement of flowers upon that stem, and in
the joining of the leaves to create an arch-
shape at the corners of the quilt.

52. 私の島

ジュニアル・D・トム作
オアフ島
1983年

　このキルトには作者の愛するハワイの自然がにぎやかに登場する。ハイビスカス、アンセリウム、ジンジャー、ジャスミンなどの花ばなに南海の魚も加わって中心部をうめ、まわりを波と飛びはねるいるかがとりかこみ、ハワイの自然というテーマそのままの楽しい作品になっている。

MY ISLAND

Juneal-Darlene Tom, maker and designer
Island of O'ahu, 1983
Plain woven cotton/polyester, hand
applique, and contour quilting
80″ (203cm.) × 110″ (279cm.)
Juneal-Darlene Tom, owner

The inspiration for My Island came to Juneal-Darlene Tom while working on another quilt. The design is based on the elements of nature which she enjoys. Represented are the ocean and its fish, flowers such as the *heliconia, pīkake*, hibiscus, anthurium, ginger, nightblooming cereus, and lemon grass from which the quilter sometimes makes tea.

The integration of these disparate motifs can be seen in the center of the quilt. Various plant species blend into one another without hesitation and the predominant use of curvilinear forms brings harmony to the overall design. The confinement of the vegetation to the center of the quilt by the surrounding fish and waves reinforces the quilt's theme and title, My Island.

現代作家の
プロフィール

Profile of
Contemporary Artists

エリザベス・アカナ

1942年生まれ、スコットランド、アイルランド、ドイツの混血
1984年：福岡で作品展示
1988年：キルト〝青の研究・愛の物語〟で受賞

Elizabeth Akana was born in Patterson, New Jersey in 1942, of Scottish, Irish, and German ancestry. After moving to Hawai'i, she received training in quilt making from Anita Henry and Meali'i Kalama, had her own quilt business, and authored *Hawaiian Quilting, A Fine Art*, published by the Hawaiian Mission Children's Society in 1981. She exhibited her quilts in Fukuoka, Japan in 1984, and received the Juliet May Fraser Award in 1988 for her quilt, A Study in Blue: A Love Story.

シャーロット・カスカート

1924年生まれ、白人とハワイアンの混血
祖母とデボラ・カカリアからキルトの手ほどきを受ける。
カワイアハオ教会、カメハメハ校、ビショップ博物館などでキルト指導
1985年　タヒチ太平洋芸術祭にハワイ州代表として出席
1988年　オーストラリア太平洋芸術祭ハワイ州代表として出席

Charlotte L. Cathcart was born in Honolulu in 1924 of Hawaiian and Caucasian ancestry. She received her training from her maternal grandmother, Maria Victor Hall, and from Deborah Kakalia. She teaches quilt making at Kawaiaha'o Church, Kamehameha Schools, and the Bernice Pauahi Bishop Museum. She was chosen as a Hawai'i representative for the Pacific Arts Festivals in Tahiti in 1985 and Australia in 1988, and she exhibited in the 1989 Asian-Pacific Exposition in Fukuoka, Japan.

メアリイ・カラマ

1909年生まれ、英国とハワイの混血祖母マリア・ナマホレからキルトの手ほどきを受ける。
カワイアハオ教会キルト教室主宰
アメリカ合衆国美術保護財団からアメリカ伝統技術保持者のタイトルを贈られる

Meali'i Kalama was born in Honolulu in 1909 of Hawaiian and English ancestry. She learned quilting from her grandmother, Maria Namahoe, and teaches regularly at Kawaiaha'o Church as well as at workshops around the state. She has been recognized by the National Endowment for the Arts as a National Traditional Artist.

キャロル・D・カマイレ

1940年生まれ
アイルランド、フランス、インド、オランダの混血
マカリリクリエーションセンターでキルト指導
1982〜88年　カマカ-カマイレハワイアンキルト展出品

Carol Dowling Kamaile was born in Los Angeles, California in 1940, and is of Irish, French, Indian, and Dutch ancestry. She teaches at McCully Recreation Center in Honolulu. She participated in the Kamaka-Kamaile Hawaiian Quilt Exhibitions from 1981 through 1988 and in 1983 was commissioned to create the quilt Mystical Rose for Honolulu's Chaminade University.

キャシー・中島

1952年マウイ島でアメリカ人の父と日本人の母との間に生まれた。3才まで美しいハワイの自然の中で育った。17才の頃から日本刺繍を学び始め、その後キルトを志す。ハワイの美しい海や緑が彼女の感性を呼び起こしたのである。俳優である夫・勝野洋の協力のもと念願のキルトスタジオKを開いたのは3年前。週に3本ものレギュラーTV番組をもち、3人の子供を育てながらのキルトづくり、彼女は日本でいちばん忙しいキルターである

Kathy Nakajima was born in Island of Maui, in 1952 of American and Japanese ancestry. As a young child, she moved with her family to Japan. At age 17 Kathy began embroidering and later taught herself Hawaiian quilting. She established Quilt Studio K in Gotemba, Japan, and has authored three books in Japanese on Hawaiian quilting. Her first book, *Hello Patchwork,* was selected as a textbook by the National School Library Textbook Selection Committee. A mother to three children, Kathy maintains a busy schedule as a quilter, TV personality and actress.

キャサリーン・P・ニシダ

1949年生まれ
ハワイ、中国、デンマークの混血
カムエラハワイアンキルトクラブのドリス・
ノサカのもとで研修
1985年～86年　ミッションハウス博物館キル
　　　ト展出品
1985年　メリーモナーク祭記念キルトとして
　　「光る海の子供たち」が受賞

　Kathleen Puanani Nishida was born in Honolulu in 1949 and is of Hawaiian, Chinese, and Danish ancestry. She received her training in quiltmaking from the Waimea Hawaiian Quilt Club (Kamuela, Island of Hawai'i) started by Doris Nosaka. She participated in exhibitions at the Mission Houses Museum in 1985 and 1986 and Hale Naua in 1987. She was the recipient of special honors in 1987 for her Merrie Monarch Festival commemorative quilt, *Kina'u Mālamalama o Ke Kai* (The Mother Sea Loves Her Children).

ロビン・K・ジェンセン

1957年生まれ
ハワイ、中国、デンマークの混血
カムエラハワイアンキルトクラブのドリス・
ノサカのもとで研修
姉キャサリーンと共に作品を展示している

　Robin Keli'i Jensen was born in Honolulu in 1957 of Hawaiian, Chinese, and Danish ancestry. He received training at the Waimea Hawaiian Quilt Club (Kamuela, Island of Hawai'i) started by Doris Nosaka. He is a co-quilter with his sister, Kathleen, and exhibits with her.

ドリス・I・F・ノサカ

1923年生まれ
ハワイ、イギリス、中国、フランス、インド
の混血
多数の私的、公的機関による作品購入
1985年　タヒチにおける太平洋美術祭に州代
表として出席
1982～83年　クック諸島、オーストラリア、
およびニュージーランドで展覧会に出品

　Doris Iwalani Feary Nosaka was born in Honolulu in 1923 of Hawaiian, English, Chinese, French, and Indian ancestry. She received her training in quilt making from Roselee Williams, Betty Lou Ho, and Meali'i Kalama. She is the founder of Ka Hui Kapa 'Āpana o Hilo (The Hawaiian Quilt Club of Hilo) and the Waimea Hawaiian Quilt Club, and she currently teaches at the Hawai'i Kamana Senior Center. She participated in the Quilter's and Embroiderer's Show in New Zealand in 1982 and in Australia in 1983, and at the Tīvaivai and Handicrafts Show in the Cook Islands in 1983. In 1985, she was chosen as a Hawai'i state representative to the Pacific Arts Festival in Tahiti.

ジュネデイレ・L・クイノリス

1937年生まれ
ハワイ、中国、ポルトガルの混血
母のマティルダ・カピナ・レボリオにキルト
の手ほどきを受ける
メリーモナークハアイアンキルト展に出品
記録映画〝ハワイアンキルト・いつくしむ伝
統〟で紹介される

　Junedale Lauwaeomakana Quinories was born in Pepe'ekeo, Island of Hawai'i, in 1937 of Hawaiian, Chinese, and Portuguese ancestry. She received training from her mother, Matilda Kapina Leborio. She participates regularly in the annual Hawaiian Quilt Exhibition of the Merrie Monarch Festival and is featured in the Hawai'i Craftsmen documentary film ''The Hawaiian Quilt: A Cherished Tradition.''

アネッテ・スマダ

1929年生まれ
日系二世
メリーモナークハワイアンキルト展およびミ
ッションハウス博物館キルト展に多数展示

　Annette Sumada was born in Wailuku, Island of Maui in 1929 of Japanese ancestry. She learned quilting in 1979 from many experienced Hilo quilters and teaches quilting in her home. She exhibits regularly in the annual Hawaiian Quilt Exhibition of the Merrie Monarch Festival and the annual Mission Houses Museum Quilt Exhibition.

ジュニアル・D・トム

1931年生まれ
白人と中国人の混血
祖母からキルトの手ほどきを受ける
1984年〝私の島〟を福岡で展示

　Juneal-Darlene Tom was born in South Dakota in 1931 of Caucasian and Chinese ancestry. She received training in quilt making from her grandmother, Mrs. Johnson, and quilts daily for commissions. She exhibited My Island in Fukuoka, Japan in 1984.

用語解説 (Glossary)

アヒナヒナ：銀の剣と呼ばれる植物

アリイ：ハワイ王族

アロハ：愛情、親愛

アマアマ：ぼら科の魚

ハラカヒキ：パイナップル

ハラオ：フラダンス、カヌーの作り方などを教えるハ
　　　　ワイの伝統的家屋

ハナイアカマラマ：月の子供たち、エマ女王の宮殿の
　　　　　　　　　名

ハウピア：ココナッツから作るプディング

フキラウ：ハワイの伝統的な魚とりの手法

イイウイ：赤いミツスイ科の鳥

イリマ：小さいハワイの黄色の花、レイに使われる

カヒリ：ハワイ王族の羽かざり

カラウヌ：王冠

カオナ：ハワイのキルトや歌などにそれとなく含まれ
　　　　るかくされた意味

カパ：ワウケの樹の内皮から作られる紙状の布

カパアパナ：アップリケのキルト

カパモエ：カパで作った寝具

カブ：神聖、禁止

クアホヌ：〝かめの背〟といわれるキルティング手法

クヒナヌイ：王と共に政治にたずさわる者

クイキラウ：コントアキルティング（デザインの輪郭
　　　　　　にそってキルティングする手法)

レフア：火の女神ペレの愛した赤い花

レイ：アロハの象徴として、首のまわり、頭上をかざ
　　　るガーランド

ロケラニ：ピンクのばら、女王エマの愛した花

ロケワイカフリ：赤とピンクの花びらを一つの花に合
　　　　　　　　わせ持つばらの花

マロロ：ハワイの飛魚

ママキ：木の名、樹皮がカパに作られる

マモ：紅花の一種、またはミツスイ科の鳥の名

モイリイ：ハワイの小魚

モキハナ：カウアイ島の島花。青い小さい実をレイに
　　　　　する

ニウ：ココナッツの木

オヒア：レフア

オオ：黒いミツスイ科の鳥

オペル：さば(魚)

パフ：フラダンスに使用するドラム

パカ：タバコの木

パパヘエナル：サーフボード

ペレ：火山の女神

ポイ：タロいもから作る食物

プアミウラナ：きんこうぼくの花

プロウロウ：棒の先にカパで包んだボールをのせ、族
　　　　　　長またはその宮殿の前において聖域立入
　　　　　　禁止の意を表す

プル：シダの葉からとれる綿状のせんい、キルトの中
　　　に入れる〝わた〟として使われた

タパ：カパ

ウアマウケエアオカアイナイカポノ：〝国土の生命は正
　　　　　　　　　　　　　　　　　義の中に守られ
　　　　　　　　　　　　　　　　　る〟1843年頃カ
　　　　　　　　　　　　　　　　　メハメハ三世に
　　　　　　　　　　　　　　　　　贈られた言葉

ウル：パンの木

ワイナ：葡萄のつる

ワウケ：木の名、樹皮から上質のカパが作られる

Glossary

'Āhinahina—The silversword (*Argyroxiphium sandwicense*), a native Hawaiian plant found particularly on Haleakalā, East Maui, and on high mountains on the Island of Hawai'i.

Ali'i—A chief or chiefess in traditional Hawaiian social structure; the nobility.

Aloha—A word with several meanings encompassing the feelings of love, affection, and charity.

'Ama'ama—A mullet fish (*Mugil cephalus*).

Halakahiki—The pineapple plant (*Ananas comosus*).

Hālau—A traditional house for instruction in such things as canoe making or hula dancing.

Hanaiakamalama—Literally, the adopted child of the moon. The name given to Queen Emma's residence in Nu'uanu Valley on the Island of O'ahu.

Haupia—A pudding made of coconut cream and a thickening agent.

Hukilau—A traditional Hawaiian method of catching fish by pulling (*huki*) on a net (*lau*).

'I'iwi—A bird, the scarlet Hawaiian honey creeper (*Vestiaria coccinea*) whose red feathers were used in traditional Hawaiian featherwork.

'Ilima—A small native Hawaiian shrub (*Sida fallax*) whose delicate flowers are strung together to make a lei, hence *'Ilima* lei.

Kāhili—A feather standard symbolic of the *ali'i*.

Kalaunu—A crown.

Kaona—A hidden or concealed meaning in many Hawaiian arts such as poetry writing and quilt pattern designing.

Kapa—A fibrous barkcloth made from pounding the inner bark of the *wauke* (*Broussonetia papyrifera*) or *māmaki* (*Pipturus albidus*) tree. Called *tapa* in other parts of Polynesia.

Kapa 'āpana—Also called *kapa lau*. A quilt with appliqued designs.

Kapa moe—Traditionally a *kapa* for sleeping. Also refers to a blanket, bedspread, or quilt.

Kapu—Sacred, prohibited. Taboo in English; *tapu* or *tabu* in other Polynesian languages.

Kuahonu—Literally means turtle back. Also the name of a quilt stitching design which, in its outline shape, resembles a turtle's back.

Kuhina nui—A co-ruler with the king.

Kuiki lau—To follow the designs in quilting; also called contour quilting.

Lehua—The red blossom of the *'ōhi'a lehua* tree (*Metrosideros collina*).

Lei—A garland of flowers worn around the head or about the neck; a symbol of *aloha*..

Lokelani—The rare double pink rose (*Rosa chinensis*) representative of the Island of Maui and a favorite blossom of Queen Emma.

Lokewaikāhuli—A type of rose which changes color from red on the outside to pink in the center.

Mālolo—A general term for Hawaiian flying fishes.

Māmaki—Small native Hawaiian tree (*Pipturus albidus*) whose inner bark is used to make *kapa*.

Mamo—A yellow-orange flower (*Carthamus tinctorius*); also the now extinct honeycreeper (*Drepanis pacifica*).

Moili'i—A little threadfish (*Polydactylus sexfilis*).

Mokihana—A slender tree (*Pelea anisata*) whose anise-scented fruits are often strung into leis. The tree is symbolic of the Island of Kaua'i.

Niu—The common coconut palm tree (*Cocos nucifera*) found throughout the tropical islands of the Pacific.

'Ōhi'a—See *lehua*.

'Ō'ō—A native Hawaiian bird, the black honeyeater (*Acrulocercus nobilis*).

'Ōpelu—The mackerel scad fish (*Decapterus pinnulatus*).

Pahu—A drum used to accompany the traditional Hawaiian hula.

Paka—The tobacco plant (*Nicotiana tabacum*) introduced to Hawai'i from tropical America.

Papa he'e nalu—A surfboard.

Pele—The Hawaiian goddess of volcanoes.

Pīkake—The jasmine flower (*Jasminum sambac*). The literal meaning is peacock and the flower was so named because Princess Ka'iulani was fond of both peacocks and jasmine.

Poi—A staple Hawaiian food made from cooked and pounded *taro* root; also made from *'ulu*.

Pua miulana—The flowers of the orange or white champak tree (*Michelia champaca*).

Pūlo'ulo'u—A *kapa*-covered ball on a stick carried before a chief as a symbol of kapu.

Pulu—Soft, glossy yellow wool on the base of tree fern leaf stalks.

Tapa—See *Kapa*

Ua mau ke ea o ka 'aina i ka pono—"The life of the land is perpetuated in righteousness;" a phrase attributed to King Kamehameha III circa 1843.

'Ulu—The breadfruit tree (*Artocarpus altilis*); also refers to the fruit from the tree. Often the first Hawaiian quilting pattern one makes.

Waina—Grapevine (*Vitis labruscana*).

Wauke—A small tree (*Broussonetia papyrifera*) whose inner bark is used to make *kapa*.

Bibliography

Akana, Elizabeth A. *Hawaiian Quilting: A Fine Art.*
   Honolulu: Hawaiian Mission Children's Society, 1981.
   "Ku'u Hae Aloha." In *The Quilt Digest II.* San Fran-
   cisco: Kiracofe and Kile, 1984.
Barrere, Dorothy B. "Hawaiian Quilting—A Way of
   Life," *The Conch Shell*, 3, no. 2 (Summer 1965).
Brigham, William Tufts. *Ka Hana Kapa: The Making
   of Bark-cloth in Hawaii.* Honolulu: Bishop Museum
   Press, 1911.
Hammond, Joyce D. *Tifaifai and Quilting of Polynesia.*
   Honolulu: University of Hawaii Press, 1986.
Inns, Helen. *How To Make Your Hawaiian Quilt.*
   Honolulu: Hawai'i Home Demonstration Council,
   1957.
Jones, Stella M. *Hawaiian Quilts.* Honolulu: Daughters
   of Hawai'i, Honolulu Academy of Arts, and Mission
   Houses Museum, 1973, rev.
Kaeppler, Adrienne L. *The Fabrics of Hawai'i (Bark
   Cloth).* London: F. Lewis, 1975.
Kakalia, Kepola. *Hawaiian Quilting as an Art.* Honolulu:
   Debora U. Kakalia, 1976.
Kerr, Marge. "Hawaiian Periwinkle," *Quilter's News-
   letter* (July/ August 1986).
Plews, Edith Rice. *Hawaiian Quilting on Kauai.* Lihue:
   Kaua'i Museum, 1976.
Schleck, Robert. *The Wilcox Quilts in Hawaii.* Lihue:
   Grove Farm Homestead and Waioli Mission House,
   1986.
Stevens, Napua. *The Hawaiian Quilt.* Honolulu: Service
   Printers, 1971.
Thurston, Lucy G. *Life and Times of Mrs. Lucy G.
   Thurston.* Honolulu: The Friend, 1934.
Tibbetts, Richard J., Jr. and Elaine Zinn. *The Hawaiian
   Quilt: A Cherished Tradition*, a 16mm film. Honolulu,
   1986.

Acknowledgements

Project Coordinator: Reiko M. Brandon, Honolulu Academy of Arts
Quilt Selection Committee:
  Reiko M. Brandon, Honolulu Academy of Arts
  Margaret S. Ehlke, Quilt Specialist
  Toni Han, Bernice Pauahi Bishop Museum
  Violet Koch, Queen Emma Summer Palace
  Lynn Martin, State Foundation on Culture and the Arts
  Lee Wild, Mission Houses Museum
  Loretta Woodard, Mission Houses Museum
  Elaine Zinn, Hawai'i Arts Council
Conservation:
  Pam Jaasko, Honolulu Academy of Arts
  Ethel Aotani, Honolulu Academy of Arts
  Jane Bassett, Pacific Regional Conservation Center
  Margaret S. Ehlke, Mission Houses Museum
  D. D. Fisk, Honolulu Academy of Arts
  Helen Friend, Honolulu Academy of Arts
  Linda Hee, Pacific Regional Conservation Center
  Florence Ikeda, Honolulu Academy of Arts
  Eva Marie Judd, Honolulu Academy of Arts
  Anne Kase, Honolulu Academy of Arts
  Amy Meeker, Honolulu Academy of Arts
  Muriel Smith, Honolulu Academy of Arts
  Jan Tagawa, Honolulu Academy of Arts
  Harriet Yamaguchi, Honolulu Academy of Arts
  Eleanor Yamasaki, Honolulu Academy of Arts
  Loretta Woodard, Mission Houses Museum
Catalogue:
  English Introduction: Lee Wild, Mission Houses Museum
  Japanese Introduction: Reiko M. Brandon, Honolulu Academy of Arts
English entries:
  Honolulu Academy of Arts Collection: Reiko M. Brandon
  Mission Houses Museum Collection: Loretta Woodard
  Bernice Pauahi Bishop Museum: Toni Han and Lee Wild
  Daughters of Hawai'i Collection: Lee Wild
  Contemporary quilts: Linda M. Le Geyt, Honolulu Academy of Arts
Japanese Entries: Reiko M. Brandon, Honolulu Academy of Arts
Photography: Tadao Kodaira
English editing: Carol Khewhok, Honolulu Academy of Arts
Insurance and shipping arrangements: Sanna Deutsch, Honolulu Academy of Arts
Packing and crate preparation: Abundio Cabe and staff, Honolulu Academy of Arts

ハワイの歴史

1778年1月18日	イギリスの探検家ジェームス・クックによりオアフ島発見。翌19日カウアイ島発見。
1795年	カメハメハ一世、ハワイ島を統一、ハワイ王国を設立。
1820年	カメハメハ王の死後、長男が二世として王位を継ぐが、王制のタブーが次第に廃止され、それによる宗教的空白にボストンからキリスト教宣教師団が布教活動に来る。
1852年	ハワイ有力産業の砂糖プラテーション経営者が国外から労働力の導入として移民の受入れを行う。中国から。
1868年(明治元年)	日本から初めてハワイへ移民が行われた。砂糖資本の政治支配が進む中、王制は、白人勢力により剝奪。
1893年(明治26年)	ハワイ王朝は終焉した。
1898年(明治31年)	スペイン・アメリカ戦争で軍事的重要性が認められて連邦議会の採決で正式に、アメリカ領土となる。
1941年(昭和16年)	日本軍の真珠湾攻撃で第2次世界大戦勃発、大戦は1945年日本の無条件降伏で終結。
1959年(昭和34年)	戦後のハワイは、人口、生産、所得とも驚異的伸展をみ、新時代に向って進んでいった。そして、時の大統領アイゼンハウアーの布告、署名により正式にアメリカの第50番目の州となる。

制作 発行	有限会社 国際アート
	東京都港区高輪1-4-26興ビル
	〒108 Tel:03-3449-6001
発行日	1989年8月18日 第1刷
	1999年9月10日 第5刷
装幀レイアウト	株式会社 ハーヴェストグラフィック
デザイン	株式会社 虹画社
写真撮影	小平 忠生
写真提供	ハワイ観光局
印刷製本	光村印刷株式会社

Co-Publisher
Honolulu Academy of Arts
900 S. Beretania Street,
Honolulu, Hawaii 96814-1495
U.S.A.
Tel. 808-532-8703
Fax. 808-532-8787

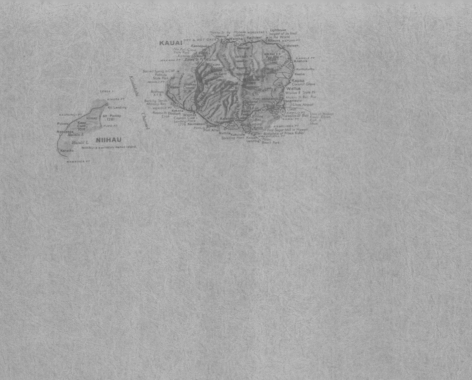

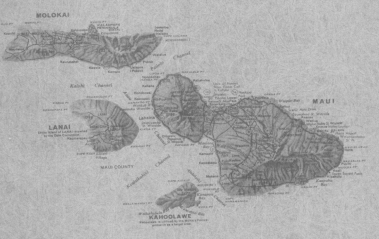